AMERICA'S JOURNAL

Considering different points of view gives us a fuller understanding of history.

SCHOLASTIC

LITERACY PLACE®

Copyright acknowledgments and credits appear on page 144, which constitutes an extension of this copyright page.

Tour
a Historical Museum

Considering different points of view gives us a fuller understanding of history.

Many Sources

We use a variety of sources to learn about history.

4

Robert Gard

Professor of Drama, University of Wisconsin

I SET OUT for the University of Kansas on a
September morning with $30 that I'd borrowed from
my local bank. I had one suit and one necktie and
one pair of shoes. My mother had spent several
days putting together a couple of wooden cases of
canned fruits and vegetables. My father, a country
lawyer, had taken as a legal fee a 1915 Buick
touring car. It was not in particularly good condition, but it was good enough to get me there. It
fell to pieces and it never got back home anymore.
I had no idea how long the $30 would last, but
it sure would have to go a long way because I had
nothing else. Fortunately, I got a job driving
left me $8 to go. The semester fee was $22; so that
for the dean of the law school. That's how
the first year
one cents, take

A Story Well Told

History can be retold in vivid ways.

WORKSHOP 2

How to Compile a Year in Review

96

THE TOP NEWS EVENTS
OF 1993–1994

OLYMPICS
PROVE
GOLDEN

In February, the world was
treated to two exciting weeks
of sport during the Winter
Olympics. The games were
held in or near the
Norwegian town of
Lillehammer. The U.S.
Winter Olympic team
collected 13 medals, its
highest total ever.

UNREST IN
RUSSIA

Fears continue that Russia
may be in for more
upheavals. President Boris
Yeltsin's reforms have created many enemies. Rising
prices, crime, and other
problems have fueled growing dissatisfaction among
political opponents as well as
the Russian public.

Many Voices

Historians compare many sources.

Trade Books

The following trade books accompany this America's Journal SourceBook.

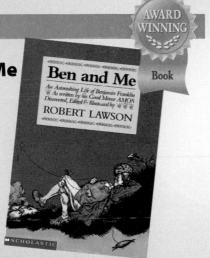

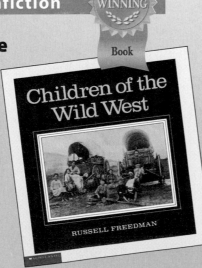
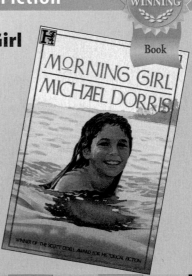

Many Sources

Travel the Oregon Trail as you read the journal of a pioneer woman. Then follow the trail on a map.

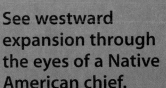

See westward expansion through the eyes of a Native American chief.

Take a ride with cowboys of the Old West. Sing a song of the *vaqueros*.

WORKSHOP 1

Learn about the past from an eyewitness when you compile an oral history.

Robert Gard
Professor of Drama, University of Wisconsin

I SET OUT for the September morning with $30 that I'd borrowed from my local bank. I had one suit and one necktie and one pair of shoes. My mother had spent several days putting together a couple of wooden cases of canned fruits and vegetables. My father, a country lawyer, had taken as a legal fee a 1915 Buick touring car. But it was not in particularly good condition, but it was good enough to get me there. It fell to pieces and it never got back home anymore.

I had no idea how long the $30 would last, but I sure would have to go a long way because I had nothing else. The semester fee was $22, so that left me $8 to go. Fortunately, I got a job driving a car for the dean of the law school. That's how I ... through the first year ... to get a pound of hamburg ... for about five cents, take ... d tracks and ...

THE W

JOURNAL OF A PIONEER

AY WEST

WOMAN
by Amelia Stewart Knight
pictures by Michael McCurdy

INTRODUCTION

This is the true story of Amelia Stewart Knight, her husband, and their seven children, who set out from Monroe County, Iowa, for the Oregon Territory in 1853. The boys were named Jefferson, Seneca, Plutarch, and Chatfield. The girls were Lucy, Frances, and Almira. The Knights started their journey in Iowa. Other families started in little towns along the Missouri River called jumping-off places because the travelers were leaving the United States and setting out through Indian Territory.

The overlanders traveled in big wagons pulled by yokes of six or eight oxen. Mrs. Knight cooked with "buffalo chips" over dusty fires. She rolled her pie dough on the wagon seat. If a family took their cows and dogs with them, the animals had to walk beside the wagons for more than a thousand miles.

A big wagon heavy with supplies could travel only ten or fifteen miles a day. It might take four to six months for a family to reach the Pacific coast. Only a few places existed on the long road where they could stop for repairs or more food. When the oxen got tired, or when the road got too rough, families lightened their loads by throwing away things they loved—rocking chairs, cradles, and even a piano might be left at the side of the road.

There were many rivers to cross on the long journey. But the people were ingenious; they painted the sides of their wagons with tar to keep water out. Then they lifted the wagon right off the flatbed and floated it across the river like a boat. They piled their belongings on the wagon bed and pushed that across the river like a raft. Indians helped the overlanders, warning them against quicksand, and trading salmon, deer meat, and moccasins for cloth and money.

When the overlanders came to the mountains, the work was different. The men pulled the wagons up to the mountaintops with winches and chains, and the women and children set rocks at the back wheels to keep the wagons from sliding down. Once they got to the top, the men tied strong rope around the wagons and pulled hard to keep them from smashing on the way down the other side.

Rain soaked through the canvas covers of the wagons, and people often became ill. Children were injured climbing on and off the moving wagons, and sometimes got lost when they strayed.

Mrs. Knight does not tell you until the very end that she is expecting another baby. You must remember her secret as you read.

LILLIAN SCHLISSEL

SATURDAY, APRIL 9, 1853. STARTED FROM HOME about eleven o'clock and traveled eight miles and camped in an old house; night cold and frosty.

MONDAY, APRIL 11, 1853. Jefferson and Lucy have the mumps. Poor cattle bawled all night.

THURSDAY, APRIL 14, 1853. Sixteen wagons all getting ready to cross the creek. Hurrah boys, all ready. Gee up Tip and Tyler, and away we go, the sun just rising.
(evening) The men have pitched the tent and are hunting something to make a fire to get supper.

SATURDAY, APRIL 16, 1853. Made our beds down in the tent in the wet and mud. Bed clothes nearly spoiled. Cold and cloudy this morning, and everybody out of humour. Seneca is half sick. Plutarch has broke his saddle girth. Husband is scolding and hurrying all hands and Almira says she wished she was home and I say ditto. "Home, Sweet Home."

THURSDAY, APRIL 21, 1853. Rained all night; is still raining. I have just counted seventeen wagons traveling ahead of us in the mud and water. No feed for our poor stock to be got at any price. Have to feed them flour and meal.

SATURDAY, APRIL 23, 1853. Still in camp. It rained hard all night, and blew a hurricane almost. All the tents were blown down, and some wagons capsized…. Dreary times, wet and muddy and crowded in the tent, cold and wet and uncomfortable in the wagon. No place for the poor children.

MONDAY, MAY 2, 1853. Pleasant evening. Threw away several jars, some wooden buckets, and all our pickles. Too unhandy to carry. Indians come to our camp every day, begging money and something to eat. Children are getting used to them.

SATURDAY, MAY 7, 1853. We have crossed a small creek, with a narrow Indian bridge across it. Paid the Indians seventy-five cents toll.

SUNDAY, MAY 8, 1853. There are three hundred or more wagons in sight and as far as the eye can reach, the land is covered, on each side of the river, with cattle and horses. There is no ferry here and the men will have to make one out of the tightest wagon bed. Everything must now be hauled out of the wagons, then the wagons must be all taken to pieces, and then by means of a strong rope stretched across the river, with a tight wagon bed attached to the middle of it, the rope must be long enough to pull from one side to the other, with men on each side of the river to pull it. In this way we have to cross everything a little at a time. Women and children last, and then swim the cattle and horses. There were three horses and some cattle drowned while crossing this place yesterday.

WEDNESDAY, MAY 11, 1853. It has been very dusty yesterday and today. The men all have their false eyes (goggles) on to keep the dust out.

FRIDAY, MAY 13, 1853. It is thundering and bids fair for rain. Crossed the river very early this morning before breakfast. Got breakfast over after a fashion. Sand all around ankle deep; wind blowing; no matter, hurry it over. Them that eat the most breakfast eat the most sand.

MONDAY, MAY 16, 1853. This afternoon it rained, hailed, and the wind was very high. Have been traveling all the afternoon in mud and water up to our hubs. Broke chains and stuck in the mud several times. The men and boys are all wet and muddy.

TUESDAY, MAY 17, 1853. I never saw such a storm. The wind was so high I thought it would tear the wagons to pieces. All had to crowd into the wagons and sleep in wet beds with their wet clothes on, without supper.

MONDAY, MAY 23, 1853. The road is covered with droves of cattle and wagons—no end to them.

TUESDAY, MAY 24, 1853. Husband went back a piece this morning in search of our dog, which he found with some rascals who were trying to keep him.

SATURDAY, MAY 28, 1853. Passed a lot of men skinning a buffalo. We got a mess and cooked some of it for supper. It was very good and tender. It is the first we have seen dead or alive.

TUESDAY, MAY 31, 1853. When we started this morning there were two large droves of cattle and about fifty wagons ahead of us, and we either had to stay poking behind them in the dust or hurry up and drive past them. It was no fool of a job to be mixed up with several hundred head of cattle, and only one road to travel in, and the drovers threatening to drive their cattle over you if you attempted to pass them. They even took out their pistols. Husband drove our team out of the road entirely, and the cattle seemed to understand it all, for they went into a trot most of the way. The rest of the boys followed with their teams and the rest of the stock. It was a rather rough ride to be sure, but was glad to get away from such a lawless set…. We left some swearing men behind us.

TUESDAY, JUNE 7, 1853. Just passed Fort Laramie and a large village of Sioux Indians. Numbers of them came around our wagons. Some of the women had moccasins and beads, which they wanted to trade for bread. I gave the women and children all the cakes I had baked. Husband traded a big Indian a lot of hard crackers for a pair of moccasins, [but when they] had eaten the crackers he wanted the moccasins back. We handed the moccasins to him in a hurry and drove away as soon as possible.

SATURDAY, JUNE 11, 1853. The last of the Black Hills we crossed this afternoon, over the roughest and most desolate piece of ground that was ever made (called by some the Devil's Crater). Not a drop of water, nor a spear of grass, nothing but barren hills.
—We reached Platte River about noon, and our cattle were so crazy for water that some of them plunged headlong into the river with their yokes on.

WEDNESDAY, JUNE 15, 1853. Passed Independence Rock this afternoon, and crossed Sweetwater River on a bridge. Paid three dollars a wagon and swam the stock across. The river is very high and swift. There are cattle and horses drowned there every day; there was one cow went under the bridge and was drowned, while we were crossing. The bridge is very rickety and must soon break down.

TUESDAY, JUNE 21, 1853. We have traveled over mountains close to banks of snow. Had plenty of snow water to drink. (Mr. Knight) brought me a large bucket of snow and one of our hands brought me a beautiful bunch of flowers which he said was growing close to the snow which was about six feet deep.

WEDNESDAY, JUNE 22, 1853. Very cold. Water froze over in the buckets; the boys have on their overcoats and mittens.

SUNDAY, JUNE 26, 1853. All hands come into camp tired and out of heart. Husband and myself sick. No feed for the stock. One ox lame. Camp on the bank of Big Sandy again.

MONDAY, JUNE 27, 1853. It is all hurry and bustle to get things in order. It's children milk the cows, all hands help yoke these cattle, the d– – –l's in them. Plutarch answers, "I can't, I must hold the tent up, it's blowing away." Hurrah boys. Who tied these horses? "Seneca, don't stand there with your hands in your pockets. Get your saddles and be ready."

WEDNESDAY, JUNE 29, 1853. The wagons are all crowded at the ferry waiting with impatience to cross. There are thirty or more to cross before us. Have to cross one at a time. Have to pay [the Indians] eight dollars for a wagon; one dollar for a horse or a cow. We swim all our stock.

SUNDAY, JULY 3, 1853. Two of our oxen are quite lame.

MONDAY, JULY 4, 1853. Chatfield has been sick all day with fever partly caused by mosquito bites.

THURSDAY, JULY 7, 1853. Our poor dog gave out with the heat so that he could not travel. The boys have gone back after him.

THURSDAY, JULY 14, 1853. It is dust from morning until night, with now and then a sprinkling of gnats and mosquitoes, and as far as the eye can reach there is nothing but a sandy desert, covered with wild sagebrush, dried up with the heat. I have ridden in the wagon and taken care of Chatfield till I got tired, then I got out and walked in the sand and through stinking sagebrush till I gave out.

SUNDAY, JULY 17, 1853. Travel over some rocky ground. Chat fell out of the wagon, but did not get hurt much.

FRIDAY, JULY 22, 1853. Here Chat had a very narrow escape from being run over. Just as we were all getting ready to start, Chatfield, the rascal, came around the forward wheel to get into the wagon, and at that moment the cattle started and he fell under the wagon. Somehow he kept from under the wheels, and escaped with only a good, or I should say, a bad scare. I never was so much frightened in my life.

SATURDAY, JULY 23, 1853. The empty wagons, cattle, and horses have to be taken further up the river and crossed by means of chains and ropes. The way we cross this branch is to climb down about six feet on the rocks, and then a wagon bed bottom will just reach across from rocks to rocks. It must then be fastened at each end with ropes or chains, so that you can cross on it, and then we climb up the rocks on the other side, and in this way everything has to be taken across. Some take their wagons to pieces and take them over in that way.

MONDAY, JULY 25, 1853. We have got on to a place in the road that is full of rattlesnakes.

THURSDAY, JULY 28, 1853. Have traveled twelve miles today and have camped in the prairie five or six miles from water. Chat is quite sick with scarlet fever.

FRIDAY, JULY 29, 1853. Chat is some better.

THURSDAY, AUGUST 4, 1853. Have seen a good many Indians and bought fish of them. They all seem peaceable and friendly.

FRIDAY, AUGUST 5, 1853. Tomorrow we will cross the Snake River. Our worst trouble at these large rivers is swimming the stock over. Often after swimming half the way over, the poor things will turn and come out again. At this place, however, there are Indians who swim the river from morning till night. There is many a drove of cattle that could not be got over without their help. By paying a small sum, they will take a horse by the bridle or halter and swim over with him. The rest of the horses all follow and the cattle will almost always follow the horses.

MONDAY, AUGUST 8, 1853. We left, unknowingly, our Lucy behind. Not a soul had missed her until we had gone some miles, when we stopped awhile to rest the cattle. Just then another train drove up behind with Lucy. She was terribly frightened and so were some more of us when we found out what a narrow escape she had run. She said she was sitting under the bank of the river when we started and did not know we were ready. And I supposed she was in Carl's wagon, as he always took charge of Frances and Lucy…. He supposed she was with me. It was a lesson to all of us.

FRIDAY, AUGUST 12, 1853. We were traveling slowly when one of our oxen dropped dead in the yoke. We unyoked and turned out the odd ox, and drove around the dead one…. I could hardly help shedding tears, and shame on the man who has no pity for the poor dumb brutes that have to travel and toil month after month on this desolate road.

WEDNESDAY, AUGUST 17, 1853. There are fifty or more wagons camped around us. Lucy and Almira have their feet and legs (covered with poison ivy).
—Bought some fresh salmon of the Indians this evening, which is quite a treat to us. It is the first we have seen.

WEDNESDAY, AUGUST 31, 1853. It is still raining this morning. The air cold and chilly. It blew so hard last night as to blow our buckets and pans from under the wagons, and this morning we found them scattered all over the valley.

THURSDAY, SEPTEMBER 1, 1853. After traveling eleven miles and ascending a long hill, we have encamped not far from the Columbia River and made a nice dinner of fried salmon. Quite a number of Indians were camped around us, for the purpose of selling salmon to the emigrants.

SATURDAY, SEPTEMBER 3, 1853. Here husband (being out of money) sold his sorrell mare (Fan) for a hundred and twenty-five dollars.

MONDAY, SEPTEMBER 5, 1853. Ascended a long steep hill this morning which was very hard on the cattle and also on myself, as I thought I never should get to the top.

FRIDAY, SEPTEMBER 9, 1853. There is a great deal of laurel growing here, which will poison the stock if they eat it. There is no end to the wagons, buggies, yokes, chains, etc., that are lying all along this road. Some splendid good wagons, just left standing, perhaps with the owners' names on them; and many are the poor horses, mules, oxen, cows, etc., that are lying dead in these mountains.

SATURDAY, SEPTEMBER 10, 1853. It would be useless for me to describe the awful road we have just passed over…. It is very rocky all the way, quite steep, winding, sideling, deep down, slippery and muddy…and this road is cut down so deep that at times the cattle and wagons are almost out of sight…the poor cattle all straining to hold back the heavy wagons on the slippery road.

TUESDAY, SEPTEMBER 13, 1853. We are in Oregon, with no home, except our wagons and tent.

SATURDAY, SEPTEMBER 17, 1853. A few days later my eighth child was born. We picked up and ferried across the Columbia River, utilizing skiff, canoes, and flatboat to get across, taking three days to complete. Husband traded two yoke of oxen for a half section of land with one half acre planted to potatoes, and a small log cabin and lean-to with no windows.

THIS IS THE JOURNEY'S END.

SOURCE

Historical
Map

OREGON

Stories of rich farmland in Oregon gave many Easterners "Oregon Fever." The rugged trail that led them there was the longest of the great overland routes used in the westward expansion of the United States. Pioneers traveled the 2,000-mile trail one step at a time.

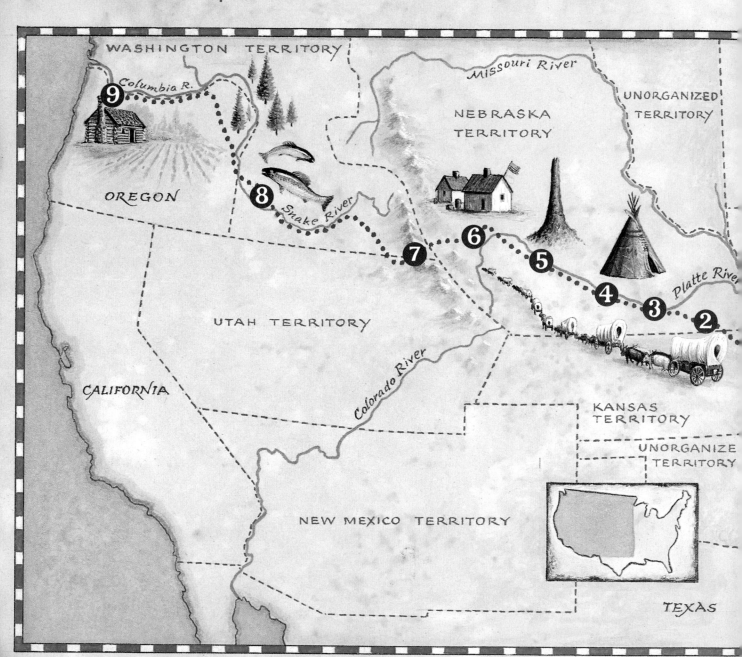

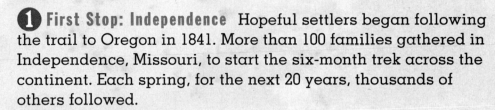

FEVER

1 **First Stop: Independence** Hopeful settlers began following the trail to Oregon in 1841. More than 100 families gathered in Independence, Missouri, to start the six-month trek across the continent. Each spring, for the next 20 years, thousands of others followed.

2 **Wagons, Ho!** The settlers joined together in wagon trains to cross the treeless plains. Wagon trains stretched for five miles and included three times more cattle and horses than people!

3 **Follow the Platte** Nebraska's chief river, the Platte, was too shallow for navigation, but settlers were able to follow its banks upstream.

4 **Native Lands** The land settlers crossed belonged to the Pawnee, Sioux, Arapaho, Cheyenne, and Crow. These Native Americans hoped the pioneers would pass through their land quickly.

5 **Chimney Rock** When settlers reached this 500-foot column of rock in the Nebraska Territory, they knew they had traveled about 550 miles. (But they still had a long way to go!)

6 **Fort Laramie** Fort Laramie was a trading post filled with useful goods such as flour, blankets, tools, rope, and water. After three months on the long trail, some people found it hard to leave.

7 **South Pass** Crossing the Rocky Mountains through South Pass was one of the most difficult parts of the trek. Stubborn cattle, plus heavy wagons, had to be hauled through treacherous ravines.

8 **The Snake River** By the fourth month, most wagon trains reached the Snake River. Its salmon-filled waters and surrounding green forests gave settlers renewed hope.

9 **Journey's End!** For most settlers arriving in the 1840s and 1850s, the journey's end was the beautiful and fertile Willamette River Valley.

Map of the Oregon Trail, circa 1853

SOURCE

Collection
of Speeches

from I HAVE SPOKEN

Orator of the Plains

by

Satanta,

KIOWA CHIEF

I love the land and the buffalo and will not part with
it. I want you to understand well what I say. Write it on
paper....I hear a great deal of good talk from the gentlemen,
but they never do what they say. I don't want any of the med-
icine lodges [schools and churches] within the country. I want
the children raised as I was....

I have heard that you intend to settle us on a reservation
near the mountains. I don't want to settle. I love to roam over
the prairies. There I feel free and happy, but when we settle
down we grow pale and die. I have laid aside my lance, bow,
and shield, and yet I feel safe in your presence. I have told
you the truth. I have no little lies hid about me, but I don't
know how it is with the commissioners. Are they as clear as I
am? A long time ago this land belonged to our fathers; but
when I go up the river I see camps of soldiers on its banks.
These soldiers cut down my timber; they kill my buffalo;
and when I see that, my heart feels like bursting; I feel sorry.
I have spoken.

Satanta, the "Orator of the Plains"

from

A LIBRARY OF CONGRESS BOOK

COWBOYS

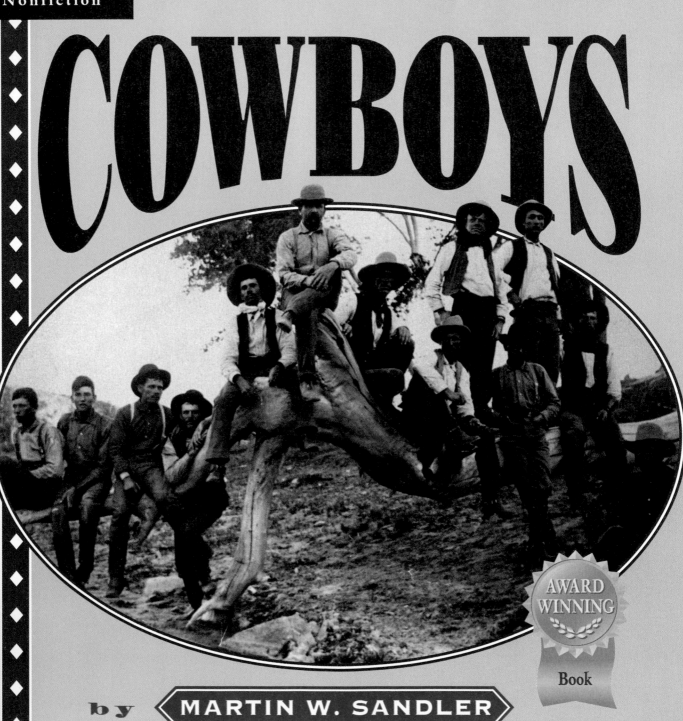

AWARD
WINNING

Book

by MARTIN W. SANDLER

An American Hero

He is perhaps the greatest of all our heroes. More songs have been written about him and more movies have been made about him than about any other figure in American history.

Since he first came on the scene, magazines and books have been filled with stories about him. Some of the stories are true. Many are not, but they add to the myths that surround him.

He is the American cowboy, and he needs no invented myths to celebrate him.

The real story is heroic enough. It is a story of men and women on horseback who turned hard work, open spaces and brave deeds into a much-envied way of life.

A Cowboy's Life

The cowboy has a tough job to do. He is in the saddle ten to fourteen hours a day. Much of his time is spent on the range tending the cattle, chasing stray steers and calves and mending fences. Each spring he is involved in rounding up the cattle, branding the calves and then leading the herds over long trails to distant markets. Most of the cowpunchers are young—in their twenties. Many are teenagers.

Everything a cowboy wears has a purpose. His wide-brimmed hat shields him from the sun and the rain. The chaps he wears over his trousers protect him from the prickly underbrush through which he rides. His high-heeled boots keep his feet from pushing through the saddle's stirrups. On the ground, his boots allow him to get a firm footing while he brings a roped steer to a halt.

The cowhand is at the center of the giant American cattle industry. Between the late 1860's and the late 1890's, the cattle he raises will supply much of the meat that will help feed a rapidly growing nation. In that brief time, more than 40,000 cowboys will raise over nine million cattle and herd them overland to far-off railroad centers. There they will be shipped to even more distant slaughterhouses and meat-packing plants.

The cowboy is a special kind of person. He is in love with nature, particularly with the great open spaces of the American West. He has a deep respect and caring for the animals around him. Above all, he places personal freedom before everything else. His way of life becomes the envy of millions of his fellow Americans, who live in crowded cities and work in stifling factories.

*Any cowboy who says he
ain't never been throwed
is a liar.*

—COWBOY SAYING

Cowboys spend most of their time on horseback, and they need to change to a fresh horse three or four times a day. Ranch owners supply the animals, but they are wild and need to be broken in. It takes several weeks and many bone-jarring sessions to tame a bucking bronco, a task that tests the courage and skill of every cowboy who attempts it.

Breaking horses is a dangerous job. On the large ranches, men called broncobusters are hired to break in the wild horses. But even these specially trained cowboys often meet with disaster. Over the years, far more cowpunchers will be seriously injured or even killed in accidents on horseback than in the more romantic gunfights that will later fill movie and television screens.

Over the years, many myths will grow up around the American cowboy. In truth, most cowboys will never see a Native American, let alone fight one. Very few will have the chance to rescue beautiful women. But one fact will not be exaggerated: The cowboys will spend their days in the saddle, and their fame as horsemen will be well deserved.

Most of the horses that the cowboys ride are descendants of animals brought to America by the Spanish. In fact, almost everything cowboys wear or use is borrowed from Spanish-speaking cattlemen called *vaqueros* who, in the late 1700's, brought their horses, cattle and skills from Mexico into Texas. It is the *vaquero* who is the true ancestor of the American cowboy.

The cowboys come from many different backgrounds. Some are veterans of the Civil War. Many are young men from the East looking for adventure, and almost all are seeking a new way of life. Many of them are African Americans. At the height of the cattle trade, more than 5,000 African-American cowboys will work on ranches, large and small, throughout the West.

Many of the African-American cowboys are ex-slaves from Texas. During their days in slavery they broke horses and herded cattle. They are excellent horsemen. Some work the ranches for a while and then find a new occupation: They become members of all-black units in the United States cavalry, where they carve out a proud record.

Many African-American cowboys are freemen from the North. Several of these cowpunchers will become famous for their riding, roping and broncobusting skills. The most famous of all will be Bill Pickett, who develops a brand-new method of throwing and holding a steer by biting into its lower lip as a bulldog might do. Thanks to him, the term "bull-dogging" becomes an important part of the cowboys' language.

I never hankered for to plow or hoe,
And punching steers is all I know.
With my knees in the saddle and
    a-hanging to the sky,
Herding dogies up in heaven in the
    sweet by-and-by.

—FROM SONG, "THE OLD CHISHOLM TRAIL"

> *Last night as I lay on the prairie*
> *And looked at the stars in the sky,*
> *I wondered if ever a Cowgirl*
> *Could get to that "Sweet By-and-By."*
>
> —From song, "The Cowgirl's Dream"

Not all the cowpunchers are men or boys; some are women. Throughout the West there are cowgirls who work the range and take part in cattle drives. Many are the wives and daughters of ranch owners. A few own their own ranches.

Cowgirls live in a man's world. They have to prove themselves every day. Those who are successful learn to ride, rope and shoot as well as their male counterparts do.

In fact, some cowgirls become even more skilled than most of the men. Before their days on the range are over, many cowgirls will be hired to show off their talents in the wild west shows that will become so popular around the world. One of the great stars of several of these shows will be Annie Oakley, who demonstrates that she can outshoot almost any man in the West. Audiences everywhere applaud the skill and daring of these hard-shooting, hard-riding women.

SONGS OF THE WILD WEST

Cielito Lindo

AWARD
WINNING

Book

The generations of easterners (and perhaps even some modern
westerners) who grew up watching William S. Hart, Tom Mix, Gene Autry,
Roy Rogers, and John Wayne in the movies and on television may find it
difficult to see cowboys as anything other than blue-eyed men with names
like McCoy, Murphy, and Jones. In fact, the pedigree of all cowboys—black,
white, brown, red—is found not in the freedom of the plains but in the
slavery of Spanish America.

When the cattle herds of the early Spanish missions had grown too large
for the priests to manage, they trained mission Native Americans—who under
Spanish colonial law were free, but for all practical purposes were enslaved to
the mission and its surrounding ranches—as horsemen. These early cowboys
were called *vaqueros*—from the the Spanish word *vaca*, meaning "cow." To
this day, a cowboy who likes to wear fancy duds and ornaments is called a
buckaroo, which is how *vaquero* sounded to Anglo ears.

By the eighteenth century, most *vaqueros* were of mixed Native American
and Spanish ancestry. They roped steers with a loop of braided rawhide called
la reata (the later cowboy's lariat) and wore leather leggings, called *chaparreras*
(chaps) to protect themselves from razor-sharp chaparral.

The "singing cowboy" of films and television could also trace his pedigree
back to the Hispanic *vaquero*. While "Cielito Lindo," a traditional Spanish
song, might have been too emotional for the stoic Anglo buckaroo, even he
would have appreciated the message of its familiar chorus: "Sing and don't cry."

Singing Vaquero
Emanuel Wyttenbach, American, 1857–1894
Brown and gray wash heightened with white

Brightly

A pronunciation guide for the Spanish lyrics appears in italics.

De la Sie - rra Mo - re - na, Cie - li - to
Day lah See-ay - rah Moe - ray-nah, See-ay - lee - toe

Lin - do vie - nen ba - jan - do.
Leen - doe bee-ay - nen bah - han - doe.

Un par de o - ji - tos ne - gros, Cie - li - to
Oon pahr day oh - hee - tohs nay - grohs, See-ay - lee - to

Lin - do, de con - tra - ban - do.
Leen - doe, day cone - trah - bahn - doe.

ENGLISH TRANSLATION:

From the Sierra Morena, Cielito Lindo, they come softly stealing.
Laughing eyes, black and roguish, Cielito Lindo, their beauty revealing.

48

CIELITO LINDO (Continued)

Ay, ay, ay, ay! Sing and don't cry,
Because singing raises the spirits, Cielito Lindo, and gladdens the heart.

How to
Conduct an Oral History

This subject was ● • • • •
interviewed about his
college experiences
during the Great
Depression.

Questions such as ●
"What did a dollar
buy?" and "What did
you do for fun?" are
always interesting
to investigate.

In some societies, history is passed down almost entirely through the spoken word. Collecting oral histories is one way that historians learn about the past.

What is an oral history? An oral history is the spoken recollections of one person. It is information about past events that has been passed on by word of mouth.

Robert Gard

Professor of Drama, University of Wisconsin

I SET OUT for the University of Kansas on a September morning with $30 that I'd borrowed from my local bank. I had one suit and one necktie and one pair of shoes. My mother had spent several days putting together a couple of wooden cases of canned fruits and vegetables. My father, a country lawyer, had taken as a legal fee a 1915 Buick touring car. It was not in particularly good condition, but it was good enough to get me there. It fell to pieces and it never got back home anymore.

I had no idea how long the $30 would last, but it sure would have to go a long way because I had nothing else. The semester fee was $22, so that left me $8 to go. Fortunately, I got a job driving a car for the dean of the law school. That's how I got through the first year.

What a pleasure it was to get a pound of hamburger, which you could buy for about five cents, take it up to the Union Pacific Railroad tracks and have a cookout. And some excellent conversation. And maybe swim in the Kaw River. One friend of mine came to college equipped. He had an old Model T Ford Sedan, about a 1919 model. He had this thing fitted up as a house. He lived in it all year long. He cooked and slept and studied inside that Model T Sedan. How he managed I will never know. I once went there for dinner. He cooked a pretty good one on a little stove he had in this thing. He was a brilliant student. I don't know where he is now, but I shouldn't be surprised if he's the head of some big corporation. (Laughs.)

1 Choose a Topic

Decide on an event or a time period that you would like to know more about. Perhaps you are interested in the first moon landing, or maybe you're curious about the 1960s in general. Make sure your topic is something that someone you know has lived through. For example, you can't record an oral history about the Civil War, which ended about 130 years ago.

TOOLS

- paper and pencil

- cassette recorder or video camera (optional)

Once you've chosen a topic, find a friend or family member who remembers it and would like to talk to you about it!

2 Prepare Questions

What do you want to know about the topic you've chosen? Make a list of the questions you'd like to have answered. Leave plenty of space after each question to jot down the answer. You may want to find out a few basic facts, such as how old your subject was during the event or era you're researching, where he or she lived, and what he or she felt was most exciting or important about the topic you chose.

3 Conduct an Interview

Collect an oral history by conducting an interview with the person you've chosen. Get the ball rolling by asking some basic questions such as those suggested in Step 2. Be sure to write down (and ask!) any new questions you think of during the interview.

Some questions may prompt long, complicated answers. Don't worry about writing them down word for word. Make note of the main points and fill in the gaps when the interview is over.

Tip Ask your subject to show you artifacts such as school yearbooks, sports memorabilia, magazines, newspaper clippings, letters, and photographs from the period you are investigating.

4 Present Your Work

Write your oral history using a question-and-answer format. Feel free to leave out any questions and answers, or parts of answers, that you feel are uninteresting or unimportant.

Share your oral history with your class. Find out if any of your class-mates collected an oral history on the same event or era you chose. Compare the two histories to find out how they are alike and how they are different.

If You Are Using a Computer ...

Draft your questions in the Journal format. After you complete your interview, write your oral history in the Newsletter format. Give it an attention-grabbing headline.

THINK

How are oral histories different from the stories you read in most history books?

Russell Freedman
Historian/Author ▶

1893

Almanack UTGIFVEN AF
AMERIKANSKA
Emigrant
KOMPANIET

OFFICES OF

THE AMERICAN EMIGRANT COMPANY

30 STATE ST. NEW YORK

LIBERTY

ELLIS
ISLAND

History can be retold in vivid ways.

A Story Well Told

Experience immigrant life in New York City at the turn of the century.

Read about Russell Freedman, a writer who brings history to life.

Meet Ellen Toliver, a fictional heroine of the American Revolution. Read a famous poem about a real-life hero.

WORKSHOP 2

Make history come alive when you compile a Year in Review.

THE TOP NEWS EVENTS OF 1993–1994

OLYMPICS PROVE GOLDEN

In February, the world was treated to two exciting weeks of sport during the Winter Olympics. The games were held in or near the Norwegian town of Lillehammer. The U.S. Winter Olympic team collected 13 medals, its highest total ever.

UNREST IN RUSSIA

Fears continue that Russia may be in for more upheavals. President Boris Yeltsin's reforms have created many enemies. Rising prices, crime, and other problems have fueled growing dissatisfaction among political opponents as well as the Russian public.

ALL SOUTH

MIDDLE EAST

55

AWARD WINNING

Book

At Home

from IMMIGRANT KIDS

by

Russell Freedman

Most turn-of-the-century immigrants settled in America's big cities. The immigrants needed jobs. The cities were growing fast and offered the best chances to find work. By 1910, three out of four people in New York City were immigrants and the children of immigrants. The same thing was true in Boston, Cleveland, Chicago, and Detroit.

Many immigrants could not speak English when they arrived. They knew little about American laws and customs. And so they clustered together, living in ethnic neighborhoods where they could mingle with their countrymen and speak their native languages. Almost every major city had its German and Irish neighborhoods, its Polish, Italian, Jewish, and Greek districts. People from the same village in Europe might wind up living as neighbors on the same street in America.

In most cities, immigrants moved into old, run-down neighborhoods. As newcomers, struggling to gain a foothold in America, they occupied the poorest and most congested districts. New York City absorbed more immigrants than any other city. Manhattan's Lower East Side, where so many immigrants settled, became one of the most densely populated places on earth.

Bargaining with a pushcart vendor

A walk through a crowded immigrant neighborhood was like a visit to the old country. The streets were noisy open-air markets. Pushcarts lined the pavements, offering fruit, vegetables, poultry, fish, eggs, soda water, and anything else you could think of—old coats for fifty cents, eyeglasses for thirty-five cents, hats for a quarter, ribbons for a penny. Peddlers hawked their wares in a dozen different dialects. Women wearing kerchiefs and shawls haggled for the best prices. Everyone except the kids seemed to be speaking a foreign language. Looking down upon these streets were the brick tenement buildings, where millions of immigrants began their lives in America.

Orchard Street on New York City's Lower East Side, 1898 (photo by Byron)

**Room in an immigrant family's tenement apartment, 1910
(photo by Jessie Tarbox Beals)**

Tenements were jammed with immigrants living in small, cramped apartments. The family shown above used a single makeshift room for cooking and eating, and as a bedroom for the kids. The parents slept in a tiny bedroom to the rear.

A more prosperous family might have three rooms: a parlor
(or living room); a kitchen; and a dark, windowless bedroom in
between. The parlor often doubled as an extra bedroom, while
the kitchen became the family's social center. In all tenements,
the toilet (or water closet) was outside the apartment, in the
hallway of the building. It was used by at least two families.

Family supper
in a tenement
kitchen (photo
by Lewis Hine)

Community water faucet in a tenement hallway (photo by Lewis Hine)

In older tenements, the individual apartments had no running water. Tenants fetched their water from a community faucet in the hallway on each floor. And yet many immigrants had grown up in the old country carrying water from a well. To them, an inside faucet with running water seemed wonderful.

Leonard Covello has described his family's first American home and his mother's reaction to running water in the hallway:

> Our first home in America was a tenement flat near the East River at 112th Street.... The sunlight and fresh air of our mountain home in Lucania [southern Italy] were replaced by four walls and people over and under and on all sides of us, until it seemed that humanity from all corners of the world had congregated in this section of New York City....
>
> The cobbled streets. The endless, monotonous rows of tenement buildings that shut out the sky.... The clanging of bells and the screeching of sirens as a fire broke out somewhere in the neighborhood. Dank hallways. Long flights of wooden stairs and the toilet in the hall. And the water, which to my mother was one of the great wonders of America—water with just the twist of a handle, and only a few paces from the kitchen. It took her a long time to get used to this luxury....
>
> It was Carmelo Accurso who made ready the tenement flat and arranged the welcoming party with relatives and friends to greet us upon our arrival. During this celebration my mother sat dazed, unable to realize that at last the torment of the trip was over and that here was America. It was Mrs. Accurso who put her arm comfortingly about my mother's shoulder and led her away from the party and into the hall and showed her the water faucet. "Courage! You will get used to it here. See! Isn't it wonderful how that water comes out?"
>
> Through her tears my mother managed a smile.

In newer tenements, running water came from a convenient faucet above the kitchen sink. This sink was used to wash dishes, clothes, and kids. Water had to be heated on the kitchen stove. Since bathing was difficult at home, most immigrants went regularly to public bath houses.

Tenement apartments had no refrigeration, and supermarkets had not yet been invented. Kids were sent on daily errands to the baker, the fishmonger, the dairyman, or the produce stall. They would rush down rickety tenement stairs, a few pennies clutched tightly in their hands. Since there were no shopping bags or fancy wrappings either, they would carry the bread home in their arms, the herring in a big pan from mother's kitchen.

Carrying home the groceries (photo by Lewis Hine)

Some immigrants had big families. (photo by Augustus F. Sherman)

Camping out on the fire escape, August, 1916

Many immigrants had to take in roomers or boarders to help pay the rent. Five or six people might sleep in one crowded room. Children were commonly tucked three and four to a bed. Privacy was unknown, and a room of one's own was a luxury beyond reach. When an immigrant family could occupy a three-room apartment without taking in boarders, they were considered a success.

On hot summer days, the stifling tenement rooms became unbearable. Whole families spilled out of their apartments, seeking relief up on the roof or down in the street, where there was some hope of catching a cooling breeze. Kids took over fire escapes and turned them into open-air clubhouses. They put up sleeping tents of sheets and bedspreads, and spent summer nights outside, as elevated trains roared past a few feet away.

Russell Freedman

Historian/Author

History writers manage *information*
about the past.

Russell Freedman is crazy about history. He studies it, he reads about it, and he has written many nonfiction books about United States history.

"History isn't just a bunch of dates and facts," Freedman says. "History is the stories of real people in real situations."

In his books, Russell Freedman brings those stories to life. How does he do it?

PROFILE

Name:
Russell
Freedman

Occupation: historian/author

Education: University of
California at Berkeley

Favorite subjects in school:
English and history

Favorite person from history:
Abraham Lincoln

Favorite childhood books:
Treasure Island,
Call It Courage

Favorite library: the
Donnell Library in
New York City

Pet: Sybil, a white cat
he rescued from the
streets of New York

QUESTIONS
for Russell Freedman

Here's how **Russell Freedman** **uncovers** the *real stories* about **past** events.

 What are the steps you take when putting together a book?

First, I research my subject. Then, I write a table of contents so that I have a clear idea of where to start and where I'm going. Next, I write five drafts of the book: a rough draft to get my ideas down, a second draft to organize the book, a third draft to cut unnecessary material, and fourth and fifth drafts' to polish my writing.

 What do you look for when you research?

 When I was researching *Cowboys of the Wild West,* for example, I relied on memoirs and diaries of cowboys. Librarians helped me find books on the subject that I hadn't read before. I also search for interesting and informative photos to illustrate my books.

 Does your research take you to interesting places?

 Frequently. Right now, I'm writing a book about Crazy Horse, a Native American chief. I've already been to Montana, to the Little Big Horn National Monument, where Crazy Horse led a famous battle against U.S. troops. I've also traveled to his homeland in the Black Hills of South Dakota.

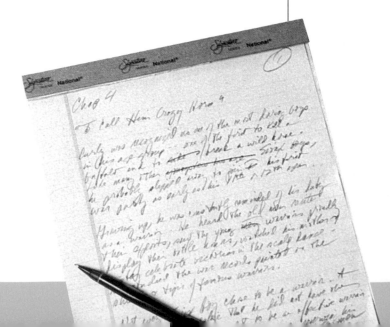

How do you choose the subjects of your biographies?

It has to be somebody that I have a compelling interest in, and that I admire for some reason. The subject's life has to really mean something.

Have kids ever inspired you to write a book?

Well, I never intended to research the Wright Brothers until so many kids asked me questions about them. That's when I decided to do a little probing. The rest is history.

How do you get readers interested in your topics?

I focus on the details of the events or people I'm writing about so they seem as real as possible.

Is it difficult to find the real story about some events in history?

Yes. The book I'm writing about Crazy Horse has been my toughest project yet. His life isn't well documented, and there are contradictory stories about how he lived.

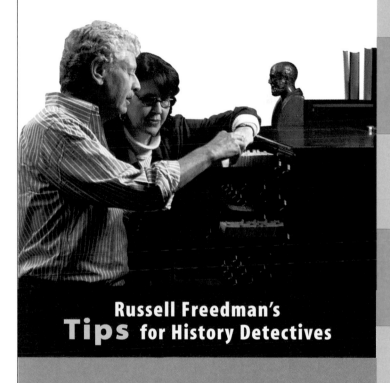

Russell Freedman's Tips for History Detectives

1 Get interested. Never write about anything you don't care about.

2 Get current. Find the newest and most authoritative books on the subject.

3 Search for details. They'll give the reader a clearer sense of what you're writing about.

4 Be suspicious. Never have fewer than three different sources for the same event.

Toliver's Secret

Historical
Fiction

AWARD
WINNING

Book

FROM TOLIVER'S SECRET

by Esther Wood Brady
illustrations by Paul Schmid

Ten-year-old Ellen Toliver knows that the American war for independence isn't an easy one. Her father has been killed in battle against the British, and her older brother is still away fighting for the Patriots. Ellen and her mother live in New York with her grandfather, a Patriot who fights against the British in his own way. He's about to carry an important message to an agent of General George Washington, when he falls and sprains his ankle. Now it's up to Ellen to deliver the message into safe hands.

"I will explain to you what this is all about," said Grandfather, "and then you can decide what to do, Ellen. I hear a lot of talk among the British officers in my shop. I hear a lot in the Tavern, too. I have information that must get to General Washington by tomorrow night at the latest. It must get there without fail. That's why I have hidden it in a loaf of bread. The bread won't attract attention, and it can be passed from one messenger to another until it gets to headquarters."

With a frown on her face, Mother jumped up from her chair and stood in front of him. "How could a message be that important, now?" she protested. "It is only two weeks until Christmas! And the officers are planning to stop the war for Christmas. I know they are."

Grandfather scowled at her. "And how could you know that, pray tell?"

"Why," said Mother, "people all over New York are having parties and balls for the officers. I hear that hundreds of fruitcakes have been made already—and thousands of candles. That's what I heard when I went to the candle shop."

Grandfather shook his head. His face, usually so pink cheeked and jolly, looked gray and drawn.

"And General Howe loves parties," Mother pressed on eagerly. "They all love parties. I know there won't be any fighting at Christmastime!"

Grandfather's eyes were grim. "Nevertheless, this message is very important! Our army has been defeated time and time again for months!" He pulled his foot from the pot of water and sat up. "Why," he exclaimed, "the British brought thirty thousand men— three times as many as Washington had!" He swung his leg over the side of the couch as if, in his eagerness to do something for Washington's army, he was ready to start.

"Whatever information we Patriots here in New York can send him about the British is important! The only way we can win is by using surprise and cunning and determination." He started to get up, but his foot touched the floor, and he groaned and fell back on the couch.

He looked at Ellen intently. "Can you understand what I have been telling you?"

"I think so."

Ellen could see that Grandfather was very serious about the need to send his message. She, too, had been worried about all the news of lost battles and retreats, especially since Ezra was with that army. She remembered how joyous everyone had been last July when they heard about the Declaration of Independence. There had been bonfires on the village green and singing and dancing in the streets. And then the British army came to New York and there had been three months of defeat.

"If you understand how important it is to take the message, Ellen, I'll tell you how it can be done. And then you are to decide."

Ellen listened and didn't say a word.

"You walk down to the docks near the Market-house and get on a farmer's boat—or an oysterman's. They come over early every morning and they go back to Elizabeth-town at eleven o'clock. Elizabeth is a very small town. When you get off the boat, you'll find the Jolly Fox Tavern without any trouble. My good friend Mr. Shannon runs the tavern, and you give the loaf of bread to him. That's all there is for you to do, Ellen. The Shannons will welcome you and take good care of you."

Sailing across the Bay didn't seem so hard. It was finding a boat here in New York and asking a stranger for a ride that worried her.

"How could I find the right boat to take me?" she asked. She didn't intend to go, but she thought she'd ask anyway.

"The docks are right near Front Street where we walked on Sunday afternoon. The farmers and the oystermen tie up their boats near the Market-house. They are friendly people and they often take passengers back to Elizabeth-town since the ferryboat stopped running. I'll give you money to pay."

"And how would I get home again—if I should decide to go?" she said in a very low voice.

"Oh, the Shannons will put you on a boat early in the morning. You'll be back here by ten o'clock."

"Does Mr. Shannon take the bread to General Washington?" she asked.

"No, he takes it to a courier who will ride part of the way. Then he'll give it to another courier who will ride through the night with it. And finally a third man will carry it to the General in Pennsylvania."

Ellen thought about the messengers riding alone through the countryside to carry the secret message. She wondered how it felt to be all alone among the British soldiers.

Mother interrupted. "It's too much to ask of her, Father. She's only ten."

Her father reached out and squeezed her hand. "Abby, dear," he said, "I know you are distressed because of all that has happened this fall. But don't make the child timid. We all have to learn to do things that seem hard at first. A child can't start too early to learn that."

Ellen knew her grandfather wouldn't send her if he thought she couldn't do it. Now that she thought it over she knew that if she walked carefully she could remember the way to Front Street. And she would have money to pay for the boat. She had liked sailing across the East River when she and Mother had taken the ferryboat from Brooklyn to New York last November. Perhaps it wouldn't be too hard. "But what would I do if I got lost?"

"If you lose your way, just speak up and ask someone for directions," said Grandfather.

"You're sure there is no one else to take it for you, Grandfather?"

"With this bad ankle I can't walk around New York to find one of my friends—and I wouldn't know where to send you or your mother to look. Besides, there isn't time. I need your help, Ellen."

Ellen was quiet for a long time.

"Very well," she said finally. "I'll do it—if you are really sure I can."

"I know you can, Ellen. And Abby," he said, "this is nothing too hard for a child of ten. The Shannons will take good care of her, you may be sure of that. In that chest in the kitchen are clothes that Ezra left here years ago. Go out and see what you find, Ellen."

Now that she had decided to go, Ellen ran quickly to the kitchen and poked around among the blankets and old clothes in the chest that sat near the fireplace. She was eager to see what was there. "Here's a striped cap," she exclaimed. "And here's that old blue jacket with the holes in the elbows. I remember these brass buttons." Grandfather had bought Ezra all new clothes when he had come to New York to visit several years ago.

Ellen put on a red knitted shirt that was too small and the blue wool jacket that was too big. The brass buttons made her think of Ezra's grin. She put on heavy gray stockings before she pulled up the short breeches. The leather breeches were so old and stiff they could almost stand alone. She kicked up her legs to make them soften up.

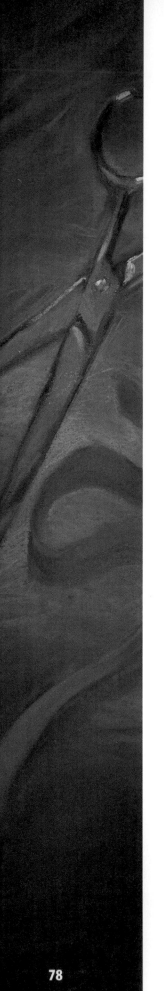

Not since she was a small child had she known what fun it was to kick her legs as high as she could. She tried to kick the skillet that hung beside the fireplace.

"These will be better for walking than petticoats," she said as she pranced about the kitchen. "Why can't girls wear these, too?"

"Ellen Toliver," said her mother primly. "It would be unseemly."

After trying on Ezra's boots, which were too big for her, she decided she would wear her own leather shoes to make walking easier. Certainly it would be easier to jump out of the way of horses and wheelbarrows and it would be better for climbing on the boat.

She ran into the shop to show her grandfather how she looked. For the first time since he fell on the ice, Grandfather laughed. "You look like a ragged little urchin all right," he said, "with those holes in your elbows. But all the better. No one will even notice you. And now we must cut your hair."

Mother picked up the scissors and stroked Ellen's long brown hair. "Couldn't we just tuck her hair under the cap?" she asked.

"No," said Ellen firmly. "I might forget and take it off! That would be dreadful. Besides, it might look bunchy beneath a cap." Better to have it short and not worry about it. She remembered her friend Lucinda who had short hair with a band of ribbon around her head. Lucinda looked very pretty with short hair. "Cut it off!" she said impatiently.

Grandfather smiled from his couch. "You'll do right well, Ellen," he said. "Tie a pigtail in back with a cord and then just snip off the part that is too long."

Ellen could feel her mother's hands tremble as she tied back the hair and snipped at the long pigtail.

"It will grow back," Ellen said to her. "How do I look?" Jumping up from the chair she stepped over the hair on the floor and stared at herself in the mirror.

"Why, I favor my father with my hair tied back!" she exclaimed. Her brown eyes were just like her father's eyes although not stern like his. Her face was thin like his, too. She stared at herself. Suddenly the person staring back at her didn't look like Ellen Toliver, and for a minute it frightened her to look so changed. Glancing sideways she could see her grandfather smiling his old cheerful smile.

Mother had given him the loaf of bread which he was wrapping in a blue kerchief and tying with a good strong knot.

"Where shall I hide the bread?" Ellen asked him.

"Don't hide it," he told her. "Don't think of hiding it. Just go along swinging this blue bundle as if it were nothing at all. There is only one thing to be careful about, Ellen. Be sure you give the bread to no one but Mr. Shannon."

His eyes grew as hard as they had been earlier that morning, when she surprised him in the kitchen. "No one but Mr. Shannon. He and I might hang if we were caught."

"Hang!" cried Ellen. "You mean on a gallows tree?"

Ellen's hands trembled so that she could hardly button the brass buttons on her jacket. No one had mentioned hanging before. If she had known her grandfather might hang she never would have agreed to do it. It wasn't fair. She gulped and at last the words came out. "I can't do it, Grandfather. I just can't. I'm too scared and I might make a mistake."

"You can do it, Ellen. Better than anyone else. No one in the world will suspect a loaf of bread in the hands of a child. If, perchance, someone found the message in the bread, just act surprised and say you don't know a thing about it!" He smiled at her to encourage her. "Just hang onto the bread good and tight until you see Mr. Shannon. That won't be hard to do, now will it?"

"But don't talk to any strangers, Ellie," Mother pleaded.

"Now, Abby. She has common sense."

"You're sure I won't make a mistake, Grandfather?"

"I can't see where you could go wrong, Ellen. The boatmen are kindly and they take people every day. And at the other end of the trip are my good friends the Shannons."

"Well, then," she said. "I think I am all ready now."

"Good!" cried Grandfather. "When you hand the bread to Mr. Shannon say this to him, 'I have brought you a present for your birthday.' He will understand what it means."

Mother slipped two corncakes into her pocket. "You'll get hungry before you get there, I'm sure." She was trying hard to sound cheerful. "I've always heard about Mistress Shannon's good potpies, and now you can eat one."

Grandfather slipped some coins into her pocket. Then he squeezed her hand until it hurt.

"God bless you, Ellen. I'm proud of you."

Mother pulled the red and white striped cap down around her ears and gave her a pair of mittens as well as a hug that almost smothered her. Then she stepped to the door and opened it. "I think you are a brave girl, Ellen."

Ellen stood at the top of the steps and looked up and down the street. She took a deep breath. Mother had said she was brave and Grandfather had said he was proud of her—well, she hoped they were right.

At first it felt strange to be walking down the same old street, looking like someone else. Ellen was sure people were watching her and wondering why she was dressed as a boy. What should she say if a woman walked up to her and asked, "Why is a girl wearing those clothes? It's not very seemly to show your legs." She'd pretend the woman had mistaken her for someone else.

But after a while, in Ezra's old breeches, her legs free of skirts and petticoats, she found it was fun to stomp along the cobblestones. She forgot what people might say. It was fun to dodge the oxcarts and the wheelbarrows and run against the wind with no cloak to hold her back. No one noticed her at all.

When she came to the pump corner she saw that Dicey and the two Brinkerhoff boys were having a snowball fight.

"That's a fair match," Ellen said to herself. She turned her head so Dicey could not see her. "Let them fight it out."

But she knew Dicey had seen her when she heard her call out, "Stop!" Ellen's heart almost stood still.

"New boy!" Dicey called. "What's your name?"

Why, Dicey didn't know her! It was just like being invisible. Dicey had looked at her and didn't know her.

Ellen peeped over her shoulder just in time to see Aaron Brinkerhoff push Dicey against a tree trunk and hold her there while Arnie gleefully scrubbed her face with handfuls of snow.

"Stop!" screamed Dicey. "Stop! Two against one ain't fair." She kicked and twisted away from them. Then, to Ellen's surprise, Dicey turned and ran away, crying like a bawling calf. Ellen stood and stared at her. For a moment she even felt sorry for her.

"Well, at least she didn't know me," Ellen said to herself. "I feel invisible."

"I'm invisible, I'm invisible," she kept saying as she ran happily down the street. Already she felt better about making the trip.

And then she felt a whack on her back that sent her spinning across the slippery cobblestones. The blue kerchief with her grandfather's loaf of bread flew from her hands.

Swift as hawks after a field mouse the two Brinkerhoff boys swooped down and snatched up her blue bundle.

"Try and get it! Try and get it!" Aaron called out. He held it out to her with an impudent grin on his face. When his brother Arnie grabbed for the bundle, Aaron snatched it away and ran. They played with it as if it were a ball, tossing it back and forth and daring her to chase them.

Ellen stood frozen with fear. What if the bread was torn apart. And the snuffbox fell out. And the British officers learned that Grandfather was a spy! It was too horrible to think of. Grandfather hanging on a gallows tree.

Her hands became fists as she thought how two laughing boys could put them all in such danger.

"Thieves!" she could hear herself shouting. "Stop those thieves!" She surprised herself by shouting those words in a loud strong voice. She surprised herself, too, by racing after the boys, dodging in and out of the crowds, tripping over children and ducking under the noses of dray horses.

"Stop those thieves!" she screamed. "They stole my bread!"

She ran up to two redcoats who stood on the steps of a bakeshop, eating hot little pies while they flirted with a group of kitchen maids.

"Please, sirs!" she gasped, "those thieves have stolen my bread!"

The soldiers shrugged and laughed. "Plenty of bread inside. The baker has just opened his ovens."

Now the boys were playing a game in front of a tailor's shop. They were tossing the blue bundle across his sign and hurling it between the wooden blades of a giant pair of scissors. Around them a crowd formed a circle to watch the fun.

"Give me my bread!" Ellen shouted as she leaped from one side to the other. She felt as nimble as a lamb without her long skirts and petticoats, but she never was quick enough to catch the bread.

Aaron mocked her. "Give the poor child his bread. He's starving!"

"Starving! Starving!" shrieked little Arnie. He held the bread out to her and then snatched it away when she jumped for it.

Two beggars watched with hungry eyes. Their bony fingers reached out to grab the bread. Even the public pig who ate scraps of garbage in the streets raced around them with greedy alert little eyes. The crowd laughed, but no one helped.

A little old woman who swept the steps of the tailor's shop with a broom of corn straw called out sharply. "What ails you Brinkerhoff boys? Always making trouble! Give the boy his loaf of bread!" She stepped down into the street and shook her broom at them. "Can't you see he's thin and hungry?"

Angrily she pushed her way through the crowd. Her back was so bent she was hardly as tall as Ellen, but she seemed to know what to do.

"Here," she said as she thrust her broom handle into Ellen's hands. "Here, trip them up. Bread is precious these days."

Ellen snatched the broomstick from the old woman. Without a moment's hesitation she raised it up and brought it down with a whack across Aaron's legs. Her eyes were blazing as she watched him duck out of her way. It made her feel good to hear him yell, "Stop," and see him dance away from her.

Arnie snatched the bundle from his brother's hands, and whirling it about his head, he grinned at her. "Try and get it!" he shrieked as he turned to push his way through the circle of people.

Ellen rushed after Arnie and whacked his legs, too. Her anger was so great she whacked at his legs until he fell sprawling on the ground.

Quick as a flash she scooped up the bundle, dropped her broom and looked for a way out of the circle.

"This way!" cried the little old woman gleefully. She held out her arms and made an opening for Ellen to get through. "Run like the wind, boy," she cried. "They'll be after you."

Ellen raced down the street. Her feet seemed to have wings. "Where to go? Where to hide?" she thought desperately as she looked over her shoulder and saw that the boys and the hungry beggars and even that awful public pig were after her.

Two boys might catch a girl who never had run on cobblestones before. But no one could catch a girl who held her grandfather's secret snuffbox in her arms.

"Stop him!" she could hear Arnie Brinkerhoff shout. "Stop the thief!"

The thief! Why, it was her loaf of bread. And why would they want it? It was just a game to them. No more important than a snowball.

She jumped over the low stone wall of a churchyard and raced across the flat gravestones. Looking back, she could see that she must have lost the beggars and the pig. Only the boys were following her. And a church warden who ran after her flapping his arms and shouting, "Be gone! Be gone!"

Over the wall she scrambled and into a street filled with haycarts going to the officers' stables. Under one cart and around another she darted. Farmers shook their pitchforks at her as she whirled past. "Don't alarm the horses!" they cried. But Ellen didn't hear them.

She had no idea where she was now as she raced around corners and down streets filled with rubble. Everywhere there were black walls of houses with roofs that had fallen in.

Gasping for breath she darted through a doorway of a broken-down house and crept into an old fireplace to hide. She was sure she had outrun the boys, but she couldn't stop the shaking of her knees. They jerked up and down like puppets on strings.

She sat down in the old ashes of the fireplace, tucked her arms around her knees and put her head on her arms. Her breath came in great sobs and blew the ashes up around her, covering her breeches with a fine dust.

"This must be the way rabbits feel—when the hounds chase them. If only I were back at home—I could crawl into bed and pull the covers over my head."

Those boys! Those horrible boys! To spoil everything at the beginning. It wasn't to have been such a long walk to Front Street. She had done it before with Grandfather.

"And now I don't know where I am," she wailed.

Grandfather had never brought her to the west side of town where the great fire burned block after block last September. It made him too sad to look at it, he said. Six hundred houses had been burned. And Trinity Church. It was lucky the whole city didn't burn up!

Slowly she began to collect her wits. Grandfather would have to find someone else to carry his message. She'd go home and tell him he had asked too much of her. She couldn't go out on the streets and roister about like a boy. She couldn't go sailing across the Bay to a place where she had never been and find a man she had never seen. That was asking too much of a ten-year-old girl. She'd go home and tell him he must find someone else.

She waited a long time to make sure the boys had not followed her. As she waited she grew calm and a strange happy feeling came over her.

She, Ellen Toliver, had fought two boys in front of a crowd of people. She not only had raced them and beaten them but she had saved her grandfather's message. The bread was here with the snuffbox still inside. She could hardly believe it.

As she sat quietly, a new feeling of confidence came to her. "Perhaps I can try to walk to the docks after all." She took a deep breath. "Perhaps I can go to Jersey after all. Grandfather said it wasn't hard. I can start over again from here, if I can find my way to Front Street."

Very carefully she crept out of the fireplace and looked around. There were tents where people must be living amidst the broken-down walls. But she saw no one around. Only stray cats that slunk away in the rubble.

"It must be getting near ten o'clock," she said to herself. There were no church bells to ring the hour, for the wardens had hidden the bells when the British came. She looked up at the hazy sun that struggled wanly in a gray sky. Grandfather always pointed out directions by the shadows the sun cast. "If the sun is on my left side—that must be the east. And the East River would be that way."

Very carefully she picked her way through the black rubble flecked with white snow. And at last she came to streets lined with fine houses and beech and sycamore trees. These streets looked familiar and the breeze had the salty fish smell of the river.

As she stepped quickly along she had a feeling the trip wouldn't be so bad after all.

from
From Sea to Shining Sea

Paul Revere's Ride

by

Henry Wadsworth Longfellow

AWARD
WINNING

Poem

illustrations by Anita Lobel

Listen, my children, and you shall hear
Of the midnight ride of Paul Revere,
On the eighteenth of April, in Seventy-five;
Hardly a man is now alive
Who remembers that famous day and year.

He said to his friend, "If the British march
By land or sea from the town tonight,
Hang a lantern aloft in the belfry arch
Of the North Church tower as a signal light,—
One, if by land, and two, if by sea;
And I on the opposite shore will be,
Ready to ride and spread the alarm
Through every Middlesex village and farm,
For the country folk to be up and to arm."

Then he said, "Good night!" and with muffled oar
Silently rowed to the Charlestown shore,
Just as the moon rose over the bay,
Where swinging wide at her moorings lay
The *Somerset*, British man-of-war;
A phantom ship, with each mast and spar
Across the moon like a prison bar,
And a huge black hulk, that was magnified
By its own reflection in the tide.

Meanwhile, his friend, through alley and street,
Wanders and watches with eager ears,
Till in the silence around him he hears
The muster of men at the barrack door,
The sound of arms, and the tramp of feet,
And the measured tread of the grenadiers,
Marching down to their boats on the shore.

Then he climbed the tower of the Old North Church,
By the wooden stairs, with stealthy tread,
To the belfry-chamber overhead,
And startled the pigeons from their perch
On the somber rafters, that 'round him made
Masses and moving shapes of shade,—
By the trembling ladder, steep and tall,
To the highest window in the wall,
Where he paused to listen and look down
A moment on the roofs of the town,
And the moonlight flowing over all.

Beneath, in the churchyard, lay the dead,
In their night-encampment on the hill,
Wrapped in silence so deep and still
That he could hear, like a sentinel's tread,
The watchful night-wind, as it went
Creeping along from tent to tent,
And seeming to whisper, "All is well!"
A moment only he feels the spell
Of the place and the hour, and the secret dread
Of the lonely belfry and the dead;
For suddenly all his thoughts are bent
On a shadowy something far away,
Where the river widens to meet the bay,—
A line of black that bends and floats
On the rising tide, like a bridge of boats.

Meanwhile, impatient to mount and ride,
Booted and spurred, with a heavy stride
On the opposite shore walked Paul Revere.
Now he patted his horse's side,
Now gazed at the landscape far and near,

Then, impetuous, stamped the earth,
And turned and tightened his saddle-girth;
But mostly he watched with eager search
The belfry-tower of the Old North Church,
As it rose above the graves on the hill,
Lonely and spectral and somber and still.
And lo! as he looks, on the belfry's height
A glimmer, and then a gleam of light!
He springs to the saddle, the bridle he turns,
But lingers and gazes, till full on his sight
A second lamp in the belfry burns!

A hurry of hoofs in a village street,
A shape in the moonlight, a bulk in the dark,
And beneath, from the pebbles, in passing, a spark
Struck out by a steed flying fearless and fleet;
That was all! And yet, through the gloom and the light,
The fate of a nation was riding that night;
And the spark struck out by that steed in his flight,
Kindled the land into flame with its heat.
He has left the village and mounted the steep,
And beneath him, tranquil and broad and deep,
Is the Mystic, meeting the ocean tides;
And under the alders, that skirt its edge,
Now soft on the sand, now loud on the ledge,
Is heard the tramp of his steed as he rides.

It was twelve by the village clock
When he crossed the bridge into Medford town,
He heard the crowing of the cock,
And the barking of the farmer's dog,
And felt the damp of the river fog,
That rises after the sun goes down.

It was one by the village clock,
When he galloped into Lexington.
He saw the gilded weathercock
Swim in the moonlight as he passed,
And the meeting-house windows, blank and bare,
Gaze at him with a spectral glare,
As if they already stood aghast
At the bloody work they would look upon.

It was two by the village clock,
When he came to the bridge in Concord town.
He heard the bleating of the flock,
And the twitter of birds among the trees,
And felt the breath of the morning breeze
Blowing over the meadows brown.
And one was safe and asleep in his bed
Who at the bridge would be first to fall,
Who at the bridge would be lying dead,
Pierced by a British musket-ball.

You know the rest. In the books you have read,
How the British Regulars fired and fled,—
How the farmers gave them ball for ball,
From behind each fence and farmyard wall,
Chasing the redcoats down the lane,
Then crossing the fields to emerge again
Under the trees at the turn of the road,
And only pausing to fire and load.

So through the night rode Paul Revere;
And so through the night went his cry of alarm
To every Middlesex village and farm,—
A cry of defiance, and not of fear,
A voice in the darkness, a knock at the door,
And a word that shall echo forevermore!
For, borne on the night-wind of the Past,
Through all our history, to the last,
In the hour of darkness and peril and need,
The people will waken and listen to hear
The hurrying hoofbeats of that steed,
And the midnight message of Paul Revere.

How to Compile a Year in Review

This review covers ● one academic (school) year, rather than a calendar (January through December) year.

Recording and categorizing historical events helps to ensure that they won't be forgotten. The most important events of each year can be recorded in a Year in Review.

What is a Year in Review? A Year in Review is a review of major events that happened during the year. Often a Year in Review covers several categories, such as sports, entertainment, and politics. At the end of each year, many newspapers, magazines, and television news programs produce Years in Review.

Photos ● illustrate some of the most dramatic moments discussed in the review.

● A title tells what type of events the Year in Review will cover.

THE TOP NEWS EVENTS OF 1993–1994

OLYMPICS PROVE GOLDEN

In February, the world was treated to two exciting weeks of sport during the Winter Olympics. The games were held in or near the Norwegian town of Lillehammer. The U.S. Winter Olympic team collected 13 medals, its highest total ever.

UNREST IN RUSSIA

Fears continue that Russia may be in for more upheavals. President Boris Yeltsin's reforms have created many enemies. Rising prices, crime, and other problems have fueled growing dissatisfaction among political opponents as well as the Russian public.

ALL SOUTH AFRICANS VOTE

South Africans cast their votes for a new government. Blacks make up 75 percent of South Africa's people. But it was the first time in the country's history that they were allowed to vote.

MIDDLE EAST PEACE AGREEMENT

For decades, Jews and Arabs in the Middle East have struggled to find some way to live in peace.

In September, the two sides took a big step toward peace. Israeli Prime Minister Yitzhak Rabin and Palestine Liberation Organization (PLO) Chairman Yasir Arafat agreed to a peace plan in Washington, D.C. "Enough of blood and tears. Enough," said Rabin.

DISASTERS ROCK THE U.S.

Relief agencies have been working around the clock to help Americans recover from a string of natural disasters.

1 Plan

Choose a year to review. You may want to examine this year and try to identify the important things that have happened so far. Or, you might choose another year, such as the year you were born. You will need to choose a topic, or several topics, to cover in your Year in Review. Some possibilities include the following:

- sports
- movies
- politics
- school and/or community events

TOOLS

- paper and pencil
- folders
- magazines and newspapers
- art supplies

2 Research

Begin your research by writing down all the important events that you remember from the year you chose. Once you've exhausted your own memory, use the library to continue your search for events. Newspapers, magazines, almanacs, videos, and computerized indexes are all helpful sources of information. Take and file notes on all of the information you've found.

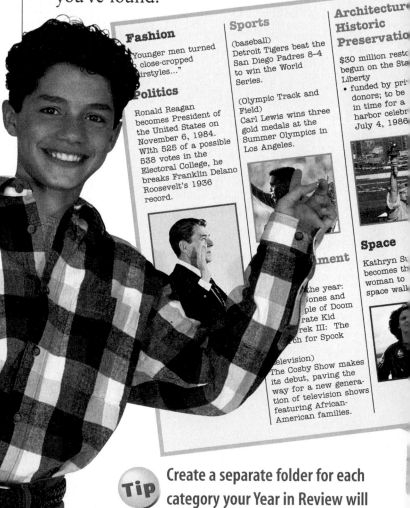

Fashion
"Younger men turned to close-cropped hairstyles..."

Politics
Ronald Reagan becomes President of the United States on November 6, 1984. WIth 525 of a possible 538 votes in the Electoral College, he breaks Franklin Delano Roosevelt's 1936 record.

Sports
(baseball) Detroit Tigers beat the San Diego Padres 8-4 to win the World Series.

(Olympic Track and Field) Carl Lewis wins three gold medals at the Summer Olympics in Los Angeles.

Architecture Historic Preservatio
$30 million resto begun on the Sta Liberty
- funded by pri donors; to be in time for a harbor celebr July 4, 1986

...ment
the year: ...ones and ...ple of Doom ...rate Kid ...rek III: The ...ch for Spock

...elevision) The Cosby Show makes its debut, paving the way for a new genera- tion of television shows featuring African- American families.

Space
Kathryn S becomes th woman to space wall

Tip Create a separate folder for each category your Year in Review will include. File your notes about each cate- gory in the appropriate folder.

3 Organize

Look through the information you've gathered. Think about how you will organize it in your Year in Review. If you have too much material, decide what's most important and delete the rest.

You may want to use one of the following organizational methods or come up with another on your own:

- Place the information in chronological (date) order.

- Make a top-five list for each category you plan to cover. Choose the five most important events in each category and include only those events.

4 Prepare and Present

Decide how to present your information. You might make a time line and illustrate it with drawings and photos. You could make a collage of clippings from various newspapers and magazines. You might even write a medley of short songs.

When you are finished, present your Year in Review to your classmates. Compare your own Year in Review to theirs. How did they present their information? How did different people cover the same years and events?

If You Are Using a Computer ...

You might want to organize your information using the Newsletter format on your computer. Create a chart or table with columns and headings for each category that you cover.

THINK

What did you learn about what makes an event important or memorable?

Russell Freedman
Historian/Author ▶

VOL. XIV......NO. 4235.

HANG OUT YOUR BANNERS

UNION

VICTORY!

PEACE!

Surrender of General Lee and His Whole Army.

THE WORK OF PALM SUNDAY.

Final Triumph of the Army of the Potomac.

The Strategy and Diplomacy of Lieut.-Gen. Grant.

Terms and Conditions of the Surrender.

Many Voices

Join Toby Hanson, as he learns about the Underground Railroad.

Find out how American history inspired a famous painter.

Meet some very young soldiers who faced a food shortage during the Civil War. Read first-hand accounts of wartime experiences.

PROJECT

Research carefully and think critically as you write a historical account.

F R O M

The House
of Dies Drear

AWARD
WINNING

Book

By VIRGINIA HAMILTON

Illustrations by KEAF HOLLIDAY

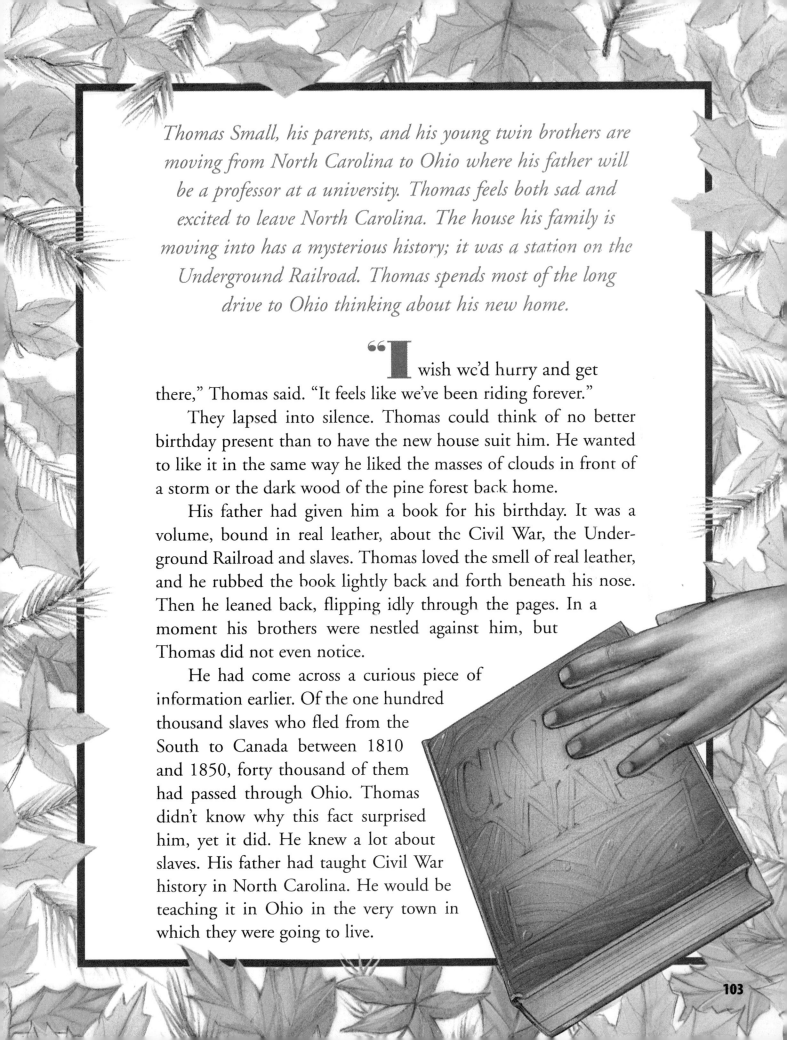

Thomas Small, his parents, and his young twin brothers are moving from North Carolina to Ohio where his father will be a professor at a university. Thomas feels both sad and excited to leave North Carolina. The house his family is moving into has a mysterious history; it was a station on the Underground Railroad. Thomas spends most of the long drive to Ohio thinking about his new home.

"**I** wish we'd hurry and get there," Thomas said. "It feels like we've been riding forever."

They lapsed into silence. Thomas could think of no better birthday present than to have the new house suit him. He wanted to like it in the same way he liked the masses of clouds in front of a storm or the dark wood of the pine forest back home.

His father had given him a book for his birthday. It was a volume, bound in real leather, about the Civil War, the Underground Railroad and slaves. Thomas loved the smell of real leather, and he rubbed the book lightly back and forth beneath his nose. Then he leaned back, flipping idly through the pages. In a moment his brothers were nestled against him, but Thomas did not even notice.

He had come across a curious piece of information earlier. Of the one hundred thousand slaves who fled from the South to Canada between 1810 and 1850, forty thousand of them had passed through Ohio. Thomas didn't know why this fact surprised him, yet it did. He knew a lot about slaves. His father had taught Civil War history in North Carolina. He would be teaching it in Ohio in the very town in which they were going to live.

He had taught Thomas even more
history than Thomas cared to know.
Thomas knew that Elijah Anderson had been
the "superintendent" of the Underground
Railroad in Ohio and that he had finally died in
prison in Kentucky. He knew that in the space of
seven years, one thousand slaves had died in Kentucky.
But the fact that forty thousand escaping slaves had fled
through Ohio started him thinking.

Ohio will be my new home, he thought. A lot of those
slaves must have stayed in Ohio because Canada was farther
than they could have believed. Or they had liked Elijah
Anderson so much, they'd just stayed with him. Or maybe
once they saw the Ohio River, they thought it was the Jordan
and that the Promised Land lay on the other side.

The idea of exhausted slaves finding the Promised Land on
the banks of the Ohio River pleased Thomas. He'd never seen
the Ohio River, but he could clearly imagine freed slaves riding
horses up and down its slopes. He pictured the slaves living in
great communities as had the Iroquois, and they had brave
leaders like old Elijah Anderson.

"Papa…" Thomas said.

"Yes, Thomas," said Mr. Small.

"Do you ever wonder if any runaway slaves from North
Carolina went to Ohio?"

Mr. Small was startled by the question. He laughed and said,
"You've been reading the book I gave you. I'm glad, it's a good
book. I'm sure some slaves fled from North Carolina. They
escaped from all over the South, and it's likely that half of them
passed through Ohio on their way to Canada."

Thomas sank back into his seat, arranging his sprawling
brothers against him. He smoothed his hand over the book and
had half a mind to read it from cover to cover. He would wake the
twins and read it all to them. They loved for him to read aloud,
even though they couldn't understand very much.

No, thought Thomas. They are tired from being up late last night. They will only cry.

Thomas' brothers were named Billy and Buster and they knew all sorts of things. Once Thomas had taken up a cotton ball just to show them about it. They understood right away what it was. They had turned toward Great-grandmother Jeffers' house. She had a patch of cotton in her garden, and they must have seen her chopping it.

They loved pine, as Thomas did, although they couldn't whittle it. Thomas' papa said the boys probably never would be as good at whittling as he was. Thomas had a talent for wood sculpture, so his father said. There were always folks coming from distances offering Thomas money for what he had carved. But Thomas kept most of his carvings for himself. He had a whole box of figures tied up in the trailer attached to the car. He intended placing them on counters and mantles all over the new house.

Thomas could sit in front of his brothers, carving an image out of pine, and they would jump and roll all around him. When the carving was finished, the twin for whom it was made would grab it and crawl off with it. Thomas never need say, and never once were the twins wrong in knowing what carving was for which boy.

They were fine brothers, Thomas knew.

If the new house is haunted, he thought, the twins will tell me!

The sedan headed through the Pisgah National Forest in the Blue Ridge Mountains, and then out of North Carolina.

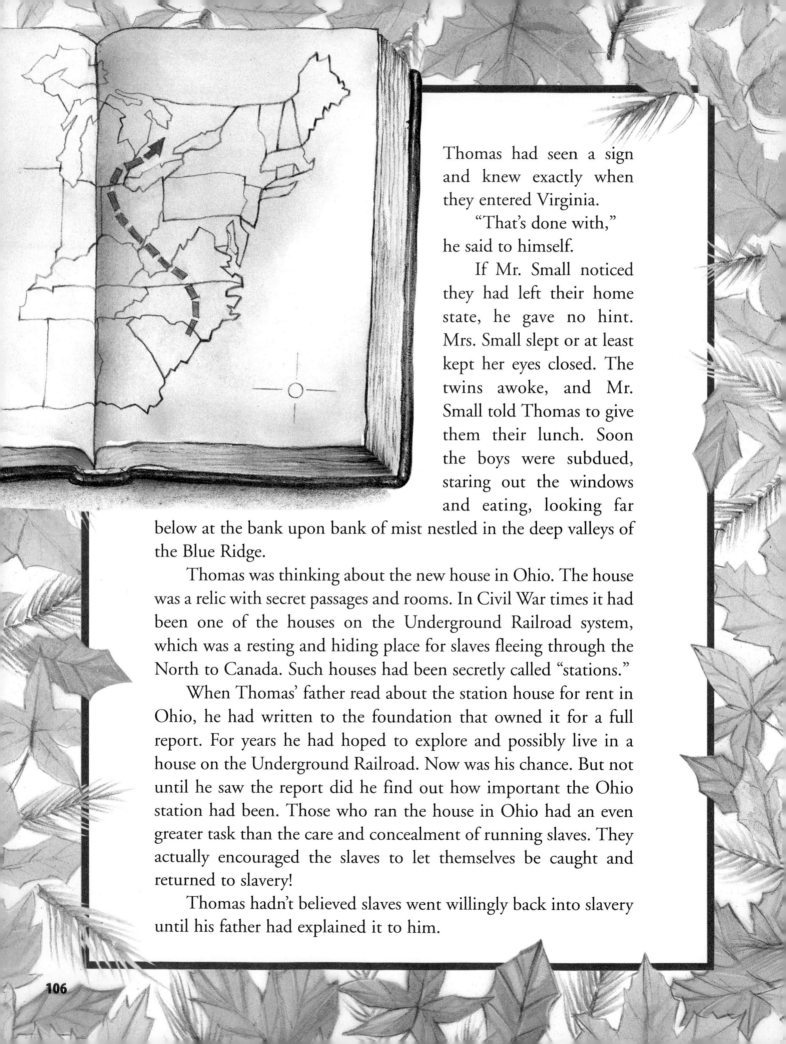

Thomas had seen a sign and knew exactly when they entered Virginia.

"That's done with," he said to himself.

If Mr. Small noticed they had left their home state, he gave no hint. Mrs. Small slept or at least kept her eyes closed. The twins awoke, and Mr. Small told Thomas to give them their lunch. Soon the boys were subdued, staring out the windows and eating, looking far below at the bank upon bank of mist nestled in the deep valleys of the Blue Ridge.

Thomas was thinking about the new house in Ohio. The house was a relic with secret passages and rooms. In Civil War times it had been one of the houses on the Underground Railroad system, which was a resting and hiding place for slaves fleeing through the North to Canada. Such houses had been secretly called "stations."

When Thomas' father read about the station house for rent in Ohio, he had written to the foundation that owned it for a full report. For years he had hoped to explore and possibly live in a house on the Underground Railroad. Now was his chance. But not until he saw the report did he find out how important the Ohio station had been. Those who ran the house in Ohio had an even greater task than the care and concealment of running slaves. They actually encouraged the slaves to let themselves be caught and returned to slavery!

Thomas hadn't believed slaves went willingly back into slavery until his father had explained it to him.

"If you'll recall your history, Thomas, you'll remember that the incredible history of the Underground Railroad actually began in Canada," his father had told him. Slaves who had reached Canada in the very early 1800s and established settlements there returned by the thousands to this country in order to free others. They came back for their families; they became secret "conductors" on the Underground Railroad system. And they returned to bondage hoping to free masses of slaves.

"But slaves continued to flee by whatever means," Mr. Small had said, "with or without help. Upon reaching the Railroad, they might hide in our house in Ohio, where they would rest for as little as a week. Some of them were given rather large sums of money and returned again to slavery."

"What would slaves need with money?" Thomas had wanted to know.

"Even a fleeing slave needs maneuvering money," his father had said. "He would need food and shelter and the best and safest way for him to get it was to buy it from freed Negroes."

"But the slaves connected with the house in Ohio were going back *into* slavery," Thomas had said.

"Yes," said Mr. Small. "And after they were caught and went back, they passed the hidden money on to other slaves, who would attempt to escape."

Still Thomas couldn't believe slaves could successfully hide money on themselves without having it found.

Some slaves did have their money found and taken away, his father said. It was dangerous work they were involved in. But others managed to return to bondage with the money still in their possession.

"Remember," his father had told him, "the slaves we're talking about weren't ordinary folks out for a peaceful stroll. Many had run for their lives for weeks from the Deep South. They had no idea how far they had to travel and they were armed with little more than the knowledge that moss grew only on the northern side of trees. Any who managed to get as far as Ohio and the Underground Railroad line had to be pretty brave and strong, and very clever. Most of them were young, with a wonderful, fierce desire to free themselves as well as others. It was the best of these who volunteered to return to slavery. They were hand-picked by Dies Drear himself, the abolitionist who built our house in Ohio. He alone conceived of the daring plan of returning numbers of slaves to the South with sizable amounts of money hidden on them."

"He must have been something!" Thomas had said.

"He was a New Englander," Mr. Small said, "so independent and eccentric, most Ohio abolitionists thought him crazy. He came from an enormously wealthy family of shipbuilders, and yet his house in Ohio was fairly modest. To give you an idea how odd he was," said Mr. Small, "his house was overflowing with fine antiques, which he neither took any interest in nor sold for profit. All the furniture remained in great piles, with just enough space to get through from room to room, until the house was plundered and Drear was killed.

"But when his plan to send slaves back to slavery worked," said Mr. Small, "there grew among freemen and slaves an enormous respect for him. You know, they never called him by his name, partly because they feared he might be caught, but also because they were in awe of him. They called him Selah. Selah, which is no more than a musical direction to raise the voice. And yet, Selah he was. *Selah*, a desperate, running slave might sigh, and the name— the man—gave him the strength to go on."

Selah. Freedom.

109

JACOB LAWRENCE

Harriet Tubman as a baby (detail)

PAINTING

Jacob Lawrence was born in Atlantic City, New Jersey, in 1917. He studied at the Harlem Art Workshop and the American Artists School in New York City. Today, he is one of America's best-known painters.

Lawrence has received many awards and honors during his long career. He served as Commissioner of the National Council of the Arts under President Carter and received the National Medal of Arts from President Bush. His work is represented in the National Gallery of Art, the Metropolitan Museum of Art, the Vatican Museum, and many other public collections.

Runaway slaves asleep in a barn

THE PAST

Harriet Tubman leads runaway slaves across the snows of the North.

The paintings shown on these pages first appeared in a picture-book biography called *Harriet and the Promised Land.* Lawrence wrote and illustrated the book to honor Harriet Tubman and her brave actions as a leader of the Underground Railroad.

Of the book, Lawrence says, "The United States is a great country. It is a great country because of people like John Brown, Frederick Douglass, Abraham Lincoln, Sojourner Truth, and Harriet Tubman.... American history has always been one of my favorite subjects. Given the opportunity to select a subject from American history, I chose to do a number of paintings in tribute to Harriet Tubman, a most remarkable woman...."

Slaves escape in a "chariot" driven by Harriet Tubman.

Harriet Tubman guides a group of escaped slaves through the woods.

A
LONG
and HUNGRY
WAR

from

~

The
Boys'
War

~

by

JIM
MURPHY

MANY OF THE SOLDIERS WHO
FOUGHT IN THE CIVIL WAR WERE BOYS, SIXTEEN YEARS OLD OR
YOUNGER. SOME OF THEM WERE AS YOUNG AS ELEVEN OR TWELVE.
THEY MANAGED TO JOIN BOTH ARMIES—UNION AND CONFEDERATE—
BY A VARIETY OF MEANS, BUT USUALLY BY SIMPLY LYING ABOUT
THEIR AGES. IN **THE BOYS' WAR,** AUTHOR JIM MURPHY
CHRONICLES THE WAR EXPERIENCES OF THE UNDERAGE SOLDIERS,
OFTEN USING FIRST-PERSON ACCOUNTS FROM THEIR LETTERS AND
DIARIES. IN THIS EXCERPT, MURPHY DESCRIBES HOW SOME YOUNG
SOLDIERS FACED FOOD-SUPPLY SHORTAGES IN THE ARMY CAMPS.

Once it was clear to both sides that they were in a real fight, one that was not simply going to fade away, some important steps had to be taken. First, many more soldiers would be needed. Second, the ragtag amateur soldiers would have to be better trained. And third, somehow, enough supplies and arms had to be found to keep the soldiers in the field.

The first two needs were reasonably easy to address. Before the first year of fighting was over, both the Union and Confederate governments issued calls for massive numbers of enlistments. These would not be ninety-day enlistments; the new soldiers would be signing on for three years! An estimated 2,898,304 would serve in the Union army during the war, while the Confederate side would see almost 1,500,000 join.

Creating good soldiers began with the officers. Many men had become officers through political favoritism or because they had been able to sign up enough recruits to make a regiment. Others were elected by the soldiers themselves, usually because they were popular, easygoing fellows. Such officers did not know how to handle groups of men during battle and never earned their respect, either.

The Union moved quickly to weed out these weak officers. Military boards were set up to examine officers, and over the next few months hundreds of officers were discharged or resigned. This did not put a complete end to the practice of appointing or electing officers, but it did establish some minimum standards for competence.

The South seemed to have gotten a better crop of officers from the start. Why did this happen? One reason is that of the eight military schools the country had in 1860, seven were located in the South. Generally, officers remained loyal to the regions where they were trained. Of the 1,900 men who had attended Virginia Military Academy, over 1,750 would serve for the South. This does not mean that every officer in the Confedcrate army was a seasoned veteran. One very young officer wrote, "While here at Taylorsville we have daily evening battalion drills, of which I know nothing in the world. In vain do I take Harder's Tactics in hand and try to study out the maneuvers."

It was not at all unusual to see large formations of soldiers being drilled by an officer with his manual of instructions firmly in hand. But as the officers learned their duties, so did the soldiers.

EDWIN FRANCIS
JENNISON,
AGE 16

~

Jennison served as a private in a Georgia infantry regiment. He was killed in battle at Malvern Hill, Virginia, in July 1862.

~

THE COOKS AT AN ARMY CAMP PREPARE TO SERVE A HOT MEAL.

The one problem neither side quite solved was how to supply their troops with enough food. A few statistics will show the immense size of the problem faced by each side. An army of 100,000 soldiers required 2,500 supply wagons and at least 35,000 horses and mules (for use by the cavalry and to haul the wagons and artillery). Men and horses consumed 600 tons of supplies *every day*!

Food had to be gathered from various growing regions and then shipped hundreds of miles by train to supply bases. Then it had to be loaded into wagons and brought to the troops in the field. As these full wagons were moving in, empty wagons had to be on the way back to the supply depots to load up the next day's supplies. All of this movement had to be timed and

BECAUSE SUPPLIES WERE GENERALLY SCARCE, A REGIMENT WAS ALLOWED A SPECIFIC AMOUNT OF EACH ITEM. HERE LOAVES OF BREAD ARE WEIGHED BEFORE DISTRIBUTION TO THE TROOPS.

carried out with precision if soldiers were going to be fed on time.

After a fumbling first year, both the Union and Confederate armies managed to organize and coordinate their supply efforts. And they worked reasonably well for the most part. Young Thomas Galway seemed pleased with his rations: "The food issued to the soldiers is very good and in ample quantity. It consists of salt pork or fresh beef; soft bread baked in field ovens, and hardtack on the march and in campaign; coffee and sugar; for vegetables, desiccated potatoes; mixed desiccated vegetables for soup; and beans, rice, and onions. Besides these, we can buy from the sutler all sorts of delicacies such as oysters, canned fruit, cheese, (and) raisins...."

But the food-supply system was a delicate ballet of movement that could be disrupted by any one of a number of things. Spring rains might turn the dirt roads into a quagmire of mud that could delay wagons for several days. A sudden movement of troops might put them in an area without adequate roads, cutting them off from supplies for days or weeks. One sixteen-year-old soldier from New York, Charles Nott, tells about his regiment's troubles during a particularly cold winter: "Again we sat down beside [the campfire] for supper. It consisted of hard pilot-bread, raw pork and coffee. The coffee you probably would not recognize in New York. Boiled in an open kettle, and about the color of a brownstone front, it was nevertheless...the only warm thing we had. The pork was frozen, and the water in the canteens solid ice, so we had to hold them over the fire when we wanted a drink. No one had plates or spoons, knives or forks, cups or saucers. We cut off the frozen pork with our pocket knives, and one tin cup from which each took a drink in turn, served the coffee."

WILLIAM
BLACK,
AGE 12

*Black
was the
youngest
known soldier
to be wounded
in the
Civil War.*

Another common complaint among soldiers was that the food they did get was almost always the same—a never-ending diet of salt pork, dried beef, beans, potatoes, turnips, and corn. After eating army food for nearly three years, Frank Carruth wrote to his sister: "I want Pa to be certain and buy wheat enough to do us plentifully—for if the war closes and I get to come home I never intend to chew any more cornbread."

Luxuries such as eggs, milk, butter, wheat flour, and sugar were scarce at the best of times and often absent for months. No wonder that one boy, R.O.B. Morrow, could write with such enthusiasm about this meal: "We are now permitted to get something to eat. I ran into a store, got hold of a tin wash pan, drew it full of molasses, got a box of good Yankee crackers, sat down on the ground in a vacant lot, dipped the crackers into the molasses, and ate the best meal I ever had."

Stores weren't always handy, especially in the wilderness areas. At these times, soldiers could buy things from sutlers. Sutlers were not an official part of the military, but they were permitted to trail after troops and sell things like food, razor blades, paper, and thread. Sutlers acquired these hard-to-come-by items directly from the manufacturers or through European sources. Often, they bought stolen goods and then charged soldiers two or three times the original purchase price. At one point in the war, eggs were selling for six dollars a dozen and bacon cost fifteen dollars a pound!

Sutlers not only charged high prices, sometimes they would refuse to sell food to soldiers they did not know or did not like. Whenever this happened, the young soldiers would find other ways to get a meal. Elisha Stockwell took great delight in outwitting one greedy sutler: "[Ed] saw him put a big sweet potato in one of the wagons, and on the way back he got that potato. It was so long he couldn't hide it in his haversack, so he put the haversack on under his coat, and in camp asked me if I could hide it. I said yes, made a hole in the middle of the fire and covered it with ashes and coals, and we waited till all had laid down [to go to sleep]. We dug it out, it was baked fine and we had all we could eat that night and the next morning." How did Stockwell feel about eating stolen food? Apparently not bad at all. "That was the best as well as the biggest potato I ever saw."

Whether it was in a letter home or a journal, food was probably the most written-about topic. Soldiers were constantly waiting for food supplies to show up or commenting unhappily about the quality, quantity, and variety when they did arrive. At times like this, soldiers often resorted to foraging to supplement their disappointing meals.

SOLDIERS LINE UP TO BUY SUPPLIES FROM A SUTLER.

F

ORAGING SIMPLY MEANT LIVING OFF THE LAND AROUND THEM.
At times, they might hunt deer or bear in the nearby forest, or gather nuts and berries. But these activities took a great deal of time, something a marching soldier did not have. Instead, soldiers had to take a more direct approach to finding a meal— they walked up to a farmer's home and offered to buy whatever food was available. If their request was refused, they would take what they wanted, sometimes at gunpoint.

Both armies had strict rules against foraging, and those caught could find themselves in jail for anywhere from a week to a month. But threats of going to jail did not put a halt to foraging. In fact, when guards were set out at night, they were there to keep soldiers *in* camp as much as to watch for an enemy attack. Still, a hungry boy could always find a way through even the tightest security, as John Delhaney makes clear: "Another nightly occupation is to rob bee hives; and not infrequently when the chorus of [religious] hymns is ascending, parties return from a thieving expedition with hats filled with honey comb."

Finding food was a constant challenge for boys in the Civil War even when safely in camp. Imagine what Charles Nott must have felt after his company became lost in enemy territory and ran out of food. After they had wandered aimlessly for several days and barely escaped capture twice, their luck changed. They stumbled across a house in the woods: "No smoke rises from the chimney. We halt; the sergeant enters the open door; comes back and reports it is just what we want—a deserted house."

After finding corn for the horses, Nott did a quick survey of their newly found bounty. In the yard, he saw chickens, cows, sheep, and pigs. Inside the house, they discovered a jar of molasses, a bag of dried peaches, a haunch of smoked venison, and a barrel of black walnuts, as well as coffee beans and cornmeal.

The food was gathered up, and after the horses had eaten, Nott and his friends continued their search for their army. That night they pitched camp and prepared a truly luxurious meal for themselves. He picks up his story: "Pluck the chickens, and cut them up; mix some meal and water, and make corn dodgers, as the Tennessians do. There are the plates to bake on, and we can try baking it in the ashes. But the coffee—everybody looks forward to it—no matter if it is poor and weak. It is always the tired soldier's great restorative, his particular comfort. The chickens must be stewed in pans and roasted on sticks."

Food for the Civil War soldier was always simple, if not downright plain. Few soldiers were skilled cooks, and even those who did know how to prepare food found themselves hampered by a lack of herbs, spices, and other ingredients. A little salt and pepper might be the only things available to put on a meal. Even so, most boys seem to have found great comfort in any meal, no matter how humble. They were able to escape, even if only for an hour or so, from the fighting and death that surrounded them. A meal was a frail link to their recollections of home and family and a better time.

Charles Nott closes his recollections of foraging with these thoughts: "In the course of half an hour we have good coffee. Chicken and corn dodgers come along more slowly, but after a while we sit around the fire to eat them; and everybody declares that he has had enough, and that it is very good."

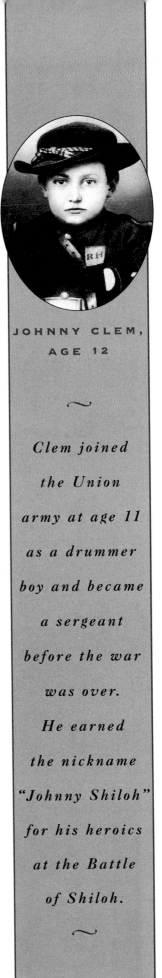

JOHNNY CLEM,
AGE 12

~

Clem joined the Union army at age 11 as a drummer boy and became a sergeant before the war was over. He earned the nickname "Johnny Shiloh" for his heroics at the Battle of Shiloh.

~

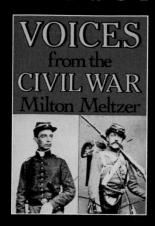

VOICES
from the
CIVIL WAR
Milton Meltzer

Document
Collection

Voices from the Civil War

A Documentary History of the Great American Conflict

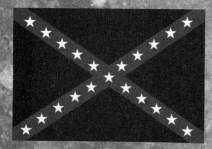

Edited by

Milton Meltzer

In the South, the Women's Relief Society was formed to collect funds and provide aid for sick and wounded soldiers. Susan Lee Blackford, a Virginian, was one of the thousands of Southern women who volunteered for nursing duty. She tells of her experience nursing wounded Confederates at Lynchburg in this letter of May 12, 1864:

May 12th

My writing desk has been open all day, yet I have just found time to write to you. Mrs. Spence came after me just as I was about to begin this morning and said she had just heard that the Taliaferro's factory was full of soldiers in a deplorable condition. I went down there with a bucket of rice milk, a basin, towel, soap, etc. to see what I could do. I found the house filled with wounded men and not one thing provided for them. They were lying about the floor on a little straw. Some had been there since Tuesday and had not seen a surgeon. I washed and dressed the wounds of about fifty and poured water over the wounds of many more. The town is crowded with the poor creatures, and there is really no preparations for such a number. If it had not been for the ladies many of them would have starved to death. The poor creatures are very grateful, and it is a great pleasure to us to help them in any way. I have been hard at work ever since the wounded commenced coming. I went to the depot twice to see what I could do. I have had the cutting and distribution of twelve hundred yards of cotton cloth for bandages, and sent over three bushels of rolls of bandages, and as many more yesterday. I have never worked so hard in all my life and I would rather do that than anything else in the world. I hope no more wounded are sent here as I really do not think they could be sheltered.

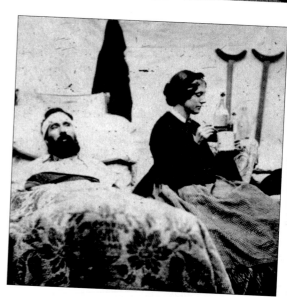

A Civil War nurse performs her duties.

Evidence of women's work for the war was gathered by Mary Livermore, a social reformer who volunteered for the Sanitary Commission in the Midwest. As she moved about collecting vast amounts of fruits and vegetables to help the Union army overcome the disease called scurvy, she saw what women could do:

Mary
Livermore

In the early summer of 1863, frequent calls of business took me through the extensive farming districts of Wisconsin, and Eastern Iowa, when the farmers were the busiest, gathering the wheat harvest. As we dashed along the railway, let our course lead in whatever direction it might, it took us through what seemed a continuous wheat field. The yellow grain was waving everywhere; and two-horse reapers were cutting it down in a wholesale fashion that would have astonished Eastern farmers. Hundreds of reapers could be counted in a ride of half a dozen hours....

Women were in the field everywhere, driving the reapers, binding and shocking, and loading grain, until then an unusual sight. At first, it displeased me, and I turned away in aversion. By and by, I observed how skillfully they drove the horses around and around the wheat field, diminishing more and more its periphery at every circuit, the glittering blades of the reaper cutting wide swaths with a rapid, clicking sound that was pleasant to hear. Then I saw that when they followed the reapers, binding and shocking, although they did not keep up with the men, their work was done with more precision and nicety, and their sheaves had an artistic finish that those lacked made by the men. So I said to myself, "They are worthy women, and deserve praise: their husbands are probably too poor to hire help, and, like the 'helpmeets' God designed them to be, they have girt themselves to this work—and they are doing it superbly. Good wives! Good women!"

One day my route took me off the railway, some twenty miles across the country. But we drove through the same golden fields of grain, and between great stretches of green waving corn. Now a river shimmered like silver through the gold of the wheat and oats, and now a growth of young timber made a dark green background for the harvest fields. Here, as everywhere, women were busy at the harvesting....

I stepped over where the girls were binding the fallen grain. They were fine, well-built lasses, with the honest eyes and firm mouth of the mother, brown like her, and clad in the same sensible costume.

"Well, you are like your mother, not afraid to lend a hand at the harvesting, it seems!" was my opening remark.

"No, we're willing to help outdoors in these times. Harvesting isn't any harder, if it's as hard as cooking, washing, and ironing, over a red-hot stove in July and August—only we have to do both now. My three brothers went into the army, all my cousins, most of the young men about here, and the men we used to hire. So there's no help to be got but women, and the crops must be got in all the same, you know."

A farm woman at work in the fields during the Civil War.

How to
Prepare a Historical Account

Use multiple *resources* to **interpret** *your* favorite piece of *history!*

A historical account is a document that contains detailed information about an event, a time period, or the achievements of an important person. When historians prepare accounts, they include plenty of well-researched facts from a variety of sources. But that's not all they must do. To prepare truly interesting accounts, historians must offer their own interpretations of history. Preparing a historical account is a good way to bring history to life!

JOHN GLENN – ASTRONAUT

FIRST TO ORBIT THE EARTH

Research a Topic

How can you learn more about a past event? You can research it, of course! Choose a topic to research. The topic might be any historical event or era that interests you. It might even be a famous person who lived long ago!

TOOLS

- paper and pencil
- note cards
- folder
- research materials

Begin your research by gathering basic information about the topic you chose. Go to the library and look for books, encyclopedias, almanacs, and magazines that tell about your topic. Check out your local video store— maybe there's a video you can use. Be sure to compare different accounts of the same event. Find as many different sources as possible. As you locate information, take notes and file them in a folder.

Tip Keep track of each source of information you use. Jot down the name of the source at the top of each note card or sheet of paper.

2 Personalize Your Research

Once you have acquired adequate knowledge of your topic, think about ways to make your account unusual and exciting. For instance, eyewitnesses are great sources of information. Is there someone you can interview who has firsthand knowledge of your topic? If your event took place a long time ago, you might search for a collection of letters, journal entries, or oral histories from people who were alive at that time. Look for magazine photos or create visual aids to illustrate your account. Perhaps you could even visit a site related to your topic and get more information there.

Make an Outline

Many historical accounts are organized chronologically—in the order that events happened. Then the reader can understand how history unfolded. Start your outline with a heading that tells what happened first and when it happened. Beneath the heading, note the important details you've collected about that particular incident. Continue with the next major item and keep going until your outline is complete. The last item on your outline should be the most recent. Remember that an outline is a way to organize your information in note form—you need not write out all your information as you will in your account.

How Am I Doing?

Before you prepare your historical account, take a minute to ask yourself these questions:

• Do I have all the information I need to write my account?

• Have I used many different sources of information?

• Have I located some unusual details?

• Have I outlined my account so that I know what to write?

4 Write Your Account

Now it's time to write your account. Try to make your topic sound exciting and fresh. Use your outline to help you write. Keep in mind that your account should be clear and interesting to read.

You might need to write several drafts before you are satisfied. Ask a classmate to read your first draft and make notes of anything he or she doesn't understand or wants to know more about. When you revise the draft, respond to your classmate's comments.

When you write your final draft, remember to leave spaces for any visual aids you plan to include. Put your historical account together in booklet form.

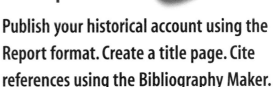

If You Are Using a Computer...

Publish your historical account using the Report format. Create a title page. Cite references using the Bibliography Maker.

5 Present Your Account

Have a History Day. Present your historical account to your classmates and share theirs. The accounts might be presented according to time period, starting with the earliest event and working up to the most recent. Look for ways that the accounts relate to one another. Did other students write about the same topic you chose? How are their accounts different from or similar to yours?

CONGRATULATIONS

You've discovered how to manage information about the past and bring a slice of history to life!

Russell Freedman
Historian/Author ▶

Glossary

ab·o·li·tion·ist
(ab′ə lish′ə nist) *noun*
A person who worked to end slavery in the United States.

ar·til·ler·y
(är til′ə rē) *noun*
Large guns mounted on wheels or on vehicles such as Jeeps.

bat·tal·ion
(bə tal′yən) *noun*
A large group of soldiers, made up of smaller companies or divisions.

bond·age
(bon′dij) *noun*
Slavery.

bri·dle (brīd′l) *noun*
The part of a horse's harness that goes over the horse's head. It is used to control or guide the horse.

bron·co
(brong′kō) *noun*
An untamed horse.

cav·al·ry
(kav′əl rē) *noun*
A group of soldiers who fight on horseback.

chap·ar·ral
(shap′ə ral′) *noun*
An area thick with shrubs and thorny bushes.

Civil War
(siv′əl wôr′) *noun*
The war between the North and the South in the United States, 1861–1865. During the *Civil War*, the United States was divided by issues such as slavery.

bronco

con·duc·tor
(kən duk′tər) *noun*
A leader of the
Underground Railroad.

con·fi·dence
(kon′fi dəns) *noun*
A powerful belief or trust
in oneself or someone else.
Getting an A on her
science test built Zoe's
confidence in herself.

cun·ning (kun′ing) *noun*
Clever or sly ways of
getting what one wants or
of escaping one's enemies.
The mouse used *cunning*
to get the cheese.

dank (dank) *adjective*
Unpleasantly damp or
humid.

de·ter·mi·na·tion
(di tûr′mə nā′shən) *noun*
Persistence; the ability to
work steadily toward a goal
until it is achieved. Jackie's
determination helped her
finish the marathon.

droves (drōvz′) *noun*
Groups of animals, such as
cows or sheep, that are
herded together from place
to place. ▲ **drove**

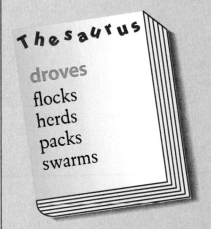

Thesaurus

droves
flocks
herds
packs
swarms

em·i·grants
(em′i grənts) *noun*
People who leave one
country to settle in another.
▲ **emigrant**

en·list·ments
(en list′mənts) *noun*
The lengths of time for
which people have joined
the military. ▲ **enlistment**

eth·nic
(eth′nik) *adjective*
Of or relating to a group of
people who have the same
national origins, language,
and culture.

fear·less
(fēr′lis) *adjective*
Brave; unafraid.

im·mi·grants
(im′i grənts) *noun*
People who come to a
new country to live.
▲ **immigrant**

Word History

Immigrant is based on
the word *migrate*, which
comes from a Latin word
meaning "to move from
one place to another."

a	add	o͝o	took	ə =	
ā	ace	o͞o	pool	ə in *above*	
â	care	u	up	e in *sicken*	
ä	palm	û	burn	i in *possible*	
e	end	yo͞o	fuse	o in *melon*	
ē	equal	oi	oil	u in *circus*	
i	it	ou	pout		
ī	ice	ng	ring		
o	odd	th	thin		
ō	open	th	this		
ô	order	zh	vision		

Glossary

in·fan·try
(in′fən trē) *noun*
A group of soldiers who have been trained to fight mainly on foot.

in·tent·ly
(in tent′lē) *adverb*
With sharply focused attention. John gazed *intently* at the questions on his history test.

lar·i·at (lar′ē ət) *noun*
A long, light rope with a sliding hoop at one end, used to catch horses and cattle; a lasso.

Word History

Lariat came from the Spanish *la reata*, which means "the rope."

---

make·shift
(māk′shift) *adjective*
Used as a temporary replacement for the usual item. The kitchen table served as a *makeshift* ironing board.

Pa·tri·ot
(pā′trē ət) *noun*
One who loves and supports his or her country.

pi·o·neer
(pī′ə nēr′) *noun*
A person who is among the first to enter or settle a region.

range (rānj) *noun*
A large area of land on which cattle and sheep graze.

re·cruits
(ri krōōts′) *noun*
People who have recently joined an organization or group such as the military.
▲ **recruit**

rick·e·ty
(rik′i tē) *adjective*
Weak and shaky.

sage·brush
(sāj′brush′) *noun*
A grayish-green bush or shrub with white or yellow flowers that grows on the dry plains in the western United States and smells like the herb sage.

sagebrush

sta·tion (stā′shən) *noun*
A regular stopping place along a route.

stir·rups (stûr′əps) *noun*
The metal or leather loops that hang from a saddle and hold a rider's feet.
▲ **stirrup**

stirrup

stock (stok) *noun*
All of the animals raised on a farm; livestock. Because of the storm, the *stock* had to be herded into the barn.

su·per·in·tend·ent
(sōōp′ər in ten′dənt)
noun
The person who is in charge of a building, organization, or project. The *superintendent* manages our apartment building.

ten·e·ment
(ten′ə mənt) *noun*
A run-down and crowded apartment building in a poor section of a city.

un·bear·a·ble
(un bâr′ə bəl) *adjective*
Intolerable; too unpleasant or distasteful to tolerate.

Un·der·ground Rail·road
(un′dər ground′ rāl′rōd′) *noun*
A system set up before the Civil War to help runaway slaves escape to the northern United States, to Canada, and to other places of safety.

va·que·ros
(vä kâr′ōz) *noun*
Latin American cowboys who worked in Mexico and the southwestern United States. ▲ **vaquero**

> **Word History**
>
> **Vaquero** comes from the Spanish word *vaca*, which means "cow."

veteran
(vet′ər ən) *noun*
A person who has served in the armed forces.

winch·es
(winch′iz) *noun*
Machines that use a chain or rope to pull or lift things. It took two *winches* to tow the car out of the mud. ▲ **winch**

winch

yoke (yōk) *noun*
A curved piece of wood that fits over a work animal's neck and is used to hitch the animal to a cart.

yoke

a	add	o͝o	took	ə =
ā	ace	o͞o	pool	a in *above*
â	care	u	up	e in *sicken*
ä	palm	û	burn	i in *possible*
e	end	yo͞o	fuse	o in *melon*
ē	equal	oi	oil	u in *circus*
i	it	ou	pout	
ī	ice	ng	ring	
o	odd	th	thin	
ō	open	th	this	
ô	order	zh	vision	

Authors & Illustrators

Esther Wood Brady *pages 72–89*
Writing historical fiction was a natural choice for this award-winning author. She grew up listening to her grandparents tell stories about her ancestors, who were early colonists. Brady began writing in 1936 and wrote many historical novels over the next four decades. She died in 1987.

Virginia Hamilton *pages 102–109*
This Newbery Medal-winning author has written many books based on her childhood in Yellow Springs, Ohio. Her grandfather, Grandpaw Levi Perry, was an escaped slave who found safety at an Underground Railroad station much like the one in *The House of Dies Drear*.

Henry Wadsworth Longfellow *pages 90–95*
This nineteenth-century poet was one of the most popular writers of his day. His poems celebrate nature, family, and American history. Few Americans of Longfellow's era knew who Paul Revere was until they read "Paul Revere's Ride."

Michael McCurdy *pages 10–29*

Writer and artist Michael McCurdy lives in Massachusetts, where he runs his own publishing company. He has written and illustrated numerous picture books, as well as illustrating classic works by authors such as Isaac Asimov, Charles Dickens, and Louisa May Alcott. His art has been shown at museums and libraries around the country.

Jim Murphy *pages 116–125*

This author says that he likes doing nonfiction projects because they allow him to investigate topics that really interest him. In researching *The Boys' War*, Jim Murphy read through hundreds of journals and letters. He went on to complete *The Long Road to Gettysburg*, another award-winning book about the Civil War.

Chief Satanta *pages 32–33*

Satanta, chief of the Kiowa tribe, was not an easy man to forget. The white settlers who came to Kiowa territory in the 1860s knew him as a powerful leader. Satanta was an eloquent speaker and often used the power of words to make peace with the settlers. But words were not enough, and Satanta led his people into war. He was sent to prison for his actions and died there in 1878.

Books &

More by Russell Freedman

Buffalo Hunt
In this book, Freedman uses beautiful historical paintings to help tell the story of the buffalo and its importance in the lives of some Native Americans.

Lincoln: A Photobiography
This Newbery-winning biography brings to life one of America's greatest presidents.

Abraham Lincoln

The Wright Brothers: How They Invented the Airplane
The story of how these inventors fulfilled their life-long dream is told through words and pictures in this book.

Kate's Book
by Mary Francis Shura
Kate and her family encounter danger and adventure when they go west in a covered wagon to start a new life in the Oregon Territory.

The Sign of the Beaver
by Elizabeth George Speare
It's 1768. Twelve-year-old Matt has been rescued from disaster by a Penobscot chief and his grandson. Now the tribe is moving on, and Matt must decide if he should go with them.

The Secret of Gumbo Grove
by Eleanora Tate
Raisen loves hearing about the past from Miss Effie, the oldest resident of Gumbo Grove. But when one of Miss Effie's stories leads Raisen to a mystery, she won't give up until she finds out whether African-American heroes once lived in her town.

And Then What Happened, Paul Revere?
by Jean Fritz
The personality and accomplishments of the Revolutionary War hero are amusingly presented in this book.

The Secret Soldier: The True Story of Deborah Sampson
by Ann McGovern
Deborah Sampson disguised herself as a man to fight in the American Revolution. Her story is detailed here.

Spanish Pioneers of the Southwest
by Joan Anderson
photographs by George Ancona
This photo essay describes life in the New Mexico territory.

Undying Glory
by Clinton Cox
During the Civil War, the 54th Regiment of Massachusetts became famous for the courage of its African-American soldiers. Here is their story.

ʁMedia

 Software

 Videos

 Magazines

The Oregon Trail
MECC
(Apple II, IBM, Mac)
As you follow in the footsteps of the pioneers you will face all the hurdles the settlers did. With some clever thinking and luck, you can make it.

Time Riders in American History
The Learning Company
(IBM)
Explore history by interviewing people from the past in this exciting game.

As the Wind Rocks the Cradle
APL Educational Video
Using diaries, journals, and memoirs, this video dramatically re-creates the experiences of five pioneer women who traveled the Oregon Trail. (60 minutes)

Forever Free (The Civil War, volume 3)
PBS/Pacific Arts
This episode of the award-winning series tells the story of the Battle of Antietam, one of the most tragic episodes in American history. (60 minutes)

Cobblestone
Cobblestone Publishing
Each issue of this magazine focuses on a specific event or person in American history. Articles, photos, folklore, games, and more bring the topic to life.

Monkeyshines on America
North Carolina Learning Institute for Fitness & Education
This playful magazine stresses state history, geography, and folklore.

A Place to Write

Association on American Indian Affairs
245 Fifth Avenue
New York, NY 10016
Include a large, self-addressed stamped envelope when you write to request an information packet about Native American history.

Acknowledgments

Grateful acknowledgment is made to the following sources for permission to reprint from previously published material. The publisher has made diligent efforts to trace the ownership of all copyrighted material in this volume and believes that all necessary permissions have been secured. If any errors or omissions have inadvertently been made, proper corrections will gladly be made in future editions.

Cover: © Edward S. Curtis/Odyssey Production.

Interior: "The Way West" from THE WAY WEST: JOURNAL OF A PIONEER WOMAN by Amelia Stewart Knight, illustrated by Michael McCurdy. Text adaptation copyright © 1993 by Simon & Schuster. Illustrations copyright © 1993 by Michael McCurdy. Reprinted by permission of Simon & Schuster Books for Young Readers, Simon & Schuster Children's Publishing Division.

Satanta, Kiowa Chief's speech and cover from I HAVE SPOKEN: AMERICAN HISTORY THROUGH THE VOICES OF THE INDIANS, compiled by Virginia Irving Armstrong, introduction by Frederick W. Turner, III. Copyright © 1971 by Virginia Irving Armstrong. Reprinted by permission of Ohio University Press/Swallow Press.

"An American Hero" and cover from COWBOYS by Martin Sandler. Copyright © 1994 by Eagle Productions, Inc. Reprinted by permission of HarperCollins Publishers.

"Cielito Lindo" and cover from SONGS OF THE WILD WEST by The Metropolitan Museum of Art. Commentary by Alan Axelrod, arrangements by Dan Fox. Copyright © 1991 by The Metropolitan Museum of Art. Reprinted by permission of Simon & Schuster Books for Young Readers, Simon & Schuster Children's Publishing Division.

"Robert Gard" selection from HARD TIMES by Studs Terkel. Copyright © 1970, 1986 by Studs Terkel. Reprinted by permission of Pantheon Books, a division of Random House, Inc.

"At Home" and cover from IMMIGRANT KIDS by Russell Freedman. Copyright © 1980 by Russell Freedman. Reprinted by permission of Dutton Children's Books, a division of Penguin Books USA Inc. Quotation within "At Home" by Leonard Covello from THE HEART IS THE TEACHER by Leonard Covello with Guido D'Agostino. Copyright © 1958 by Leonard Covello. McGraw-Hill Book Company. Reprinted by permission of Blassingame Spectrum Corp.

Selection and cover from TOLIVER'S SECRET by Esther Wood Brady. Text copyright © 1976 by Esther Wood. Cover art copyright © 1993 by Dan Andreasen. Reprinted by permission of Crown Publishers, Inc.

Cover and illustrations for "Paul Revere's Ride" from FROM SEA TO SHINING SEA, edited by Amy L. Cohn. Cover copyright © 1993 by Scholastic Inc. Illustrations by Anita Lobel, copyright © 1993 by Anita Lobel. Reprinted by permission of Scholastic Inc.

Selections from "The Top News Events of 1993-94" from Junior Scholastic, May 6, 1994. Copyright © 1994 by Scholastic Inc. Published by Scholastic Inc. Used by permission.

Selection and cover from THE HOUSE OF DIES DREAR by Virginia Hamilton. Text copyright © 1968 by Virginia Hamilton. Cover art by Eros Keith, copyright © 1968 by Macmillan Publishing Company. This edition is reprinted by arrangement with Simon & Schuster Books for Young Readers, Simon & Schuster Children's Publishing Division.

"A Long and Hungry War" and cover from THE BOYS' WAR by Jim Murphy. Text copyright © 1990 by Jim Murphy. Reprinted by permission of Clarion Books/Houghton Mifflin Co. All rights reserved.

Cover from VOICES FROM THE CIVIL WAR by Milton Meltzer. Copyright © 1989 by Harper & Row, Publishers Inc. Reprinted by permission of HarperCollins Publishers Inc.

Cover of BEN AND ME by Robert Lawson. Illustration copyright © 1939 by Robert Lawson, renewed 1967 by John W. Boyd. Published by Little Brown & Company, Inc.

Cover of THE CAPTIVE by Joyce Hansen, illustrated by John Thompson. Illustration copyright © 1993 by John Thompson. Published by Scholastic Inc.

Cover of CHILDREN OF THE WILD WEST by Russell Freedman, photograph by the Denver Public Library. Hand-tinted by Joan Menschenfreund. Photograph copyright © 1983 by Houghton Mifflin Company. Published by Clarion Books, a division of Houghton Mifflin Company.

Cover of MORNING GIRL by Michael Dorris, illustrated by Ellen Thompson. Illustration copyright © 1994 by Ellen Thompson. Published by Hyperion Books for Children.

Photography and Illustration Credits

Photos: © John Lei for Scholastic Inc., all Tool Box items unless otherwise noted. p. 2 bl, cl: © Andrew M. Levine for Scholastic Inc.; tl: © Andrew M. Levine for Scholastic Inc./Library of Congress, National Park Service-USDI, Library of Congress, Jacob A. Riis Collection, Museum of the City of New York. pp. 2-3 background: © Bob Krist/Black Star. p. 3 br: © Andrew M. Levine for Scholastic Inc. p. 4 c: © Ferguson & Katzman/Tony Stone Images Inc.; tc: © Ana Esperanza Nance for Scholastic Inc. p. 5 c, tc: © Ana Esperanza Nance for Scholastic Inc. p. 6 c, tc: © Ana Esperanza Nance for Scholastic Inc. p. 31 c: Courtesy of Smithsonian Institute Indian chief Satanta. p. 34: © Leib Image Archives. p. 35: © Library of Congress. pp. 36-39: © The Erwin E. Smith Collection of the Library of Congress on deposit at the Amon Carter Museum, Ft. Worth, TX. p. 40: © Library of Congress. p. 41 tr: © Library of Congress; bl: © Erwin E. Smith Collection of the Library of Congress on deposit at the Amon Carter Museum, Ft. Worth, TX. p. 42 bc: © Erwin E. Smith Collection of the Library of Congress on deposit at the Amon Carter Museum, Ft. Worth, TX. pp. 43-44: © Library of Congress. p. 45: © Library of Congress. p. 46 tc: The Metropolitan Museum of Art, Rogers Fund, 1979. p. 47: © "Singing Vaquero" by Emanuel Wyttenbach/The Metropolitan Museum of Art, The Elisha Whittlesey Collection, The Elisha Whittlesey Fund, 1949. p. 50 car: The Bettmann Archive. pp. 50-51: Reuters/Bettmann. p. 51 br: © John Lei for Scholastic Inc. pp. 52-53: © Jeff Isaac Greenberg/Photo Researchers, Inc. p. 53 br: © Andrew M. Levine for Scholastic Inc. p. 56 c: © National Park Service. pp. 56-57 background: © The Bettmann Archive. p. 58: © The Library of Congress. p. 59: "Orchard Street on New York City's Lower East Side," 1898/© The Byron Collection/Museum of the City of New York. p. 60: "Room in an Immigrant Family's Tenement Apartment," 1910/© Jessie Tarbox Beals/The Jacob A. Riis Collection, #502/Museum of the City of New York. pp. 61-62, 64-65: Lewis Hine/George Eastman House. p. 66: © Gift of Tenement House Dept./Museum of the City of New York. p. 67: © National Park Service. p. 68 tc: © Ana Esperanza Nance for Scholastic Inc.; all others: © Andrew M. Levine for Scholastic Inc. pp. 69-71: © Andrew M. Levine for Scholastic Inc. except for p. 71 bc: Library of Congress, Wide World Photos, Courtesy of Bancroft Library, University of CA, Berkeley. p. 96: © Tom Van Sant/The Stock Market. p. 97 Mandela: © AP/Wide World Photos; Clinton: © Les Stone/ Sygma; Jansen: © Dallas Morning News/Liaison/ Gamma-Liaison. p. 98 bc: © Stanley Bach for Scholastic Inc. Reagan: © Bettmann Archive; Lewis: © Kennerly/Gamma Liaison; Statue of Liberty: © Bettmann Newsphoto; Sullivan: © Benson/Gamma Liaison. p. 99 br: © Andrew M. Levine for Scholastic Inc. p. 110 c: Detail of "Harriet Tubman as a Baby" by Jacob Lawrence/Courtesy of Jacob Lawrence and Francine Seders Gallery, Seattle, WA. p. 111 cl: "Runaway Slaves Asleep in a Barn" by Jacob Lawrence/Courtesy of Jacob Lawrence and Francine Seders Gallery, Seattle, WA. p. 112: "Harriet Tubman Leads Runaway Slaves Across the Snows of the North" by Jacob Lawrence/Courtesy of Jacob Lawrence and Francine Seders Gallery, Seattle, WA. p. 113 cr: "Slaves Escape in a 'Chariot' Driven by Harriet Tubman" by Jacob Lawrence/Courtesy of Jacob Lawrence and Francine Seders Gallery, Seattle, WA. pp. 114-115: "Harriet Tubman Guides a Group of Escaped Slaves Through the Woods" by Jacob Lawrence/Courtesy of Jacob Lawrence and Francine Seders Gallery, Seattle, WA. p. 116: © The Bettmann Archive. p. 117 cr: © David J. Eicher/Well-Traveled Images. p. 119 bc: © Leib Image Archives; tr: © Library of Congress. p. 120 c: © The Bettmann Archive. p. 121 tr: © Library of Congress. p. 122 tl: © Library of Congress. p. 123 bc: © Leib Image Archives. p. 125 tr: © Library of Congress. p. 126 cl: © The Bettmann Archive; cr: © Leib Image Archives. p. 127 cr: © Leib Image Archives. p. 127: © Halley Ganges for Scholastic Inc. p. 128 cl: © Library of Congress. pp. 128-129: © Halley Ganges for Scholastic Inc. p. 129 cr: © Brown Brothers. p. 130 tr: © NASA; cr: © Bettmann Archive. p. 131 c: © NASA/Photo Researchers, Inc. pp. 132-133: © Stanley Bach for Scholastic Inc. p. 134 bl: © AP/WideWorld Photos; cr: © Stanley Bach for Scholastic Inc. p. 135 br: © Andrew M. Levine for Scholastic Inc. p. 136 br: © John Eastcott/Yva Momatuk/The Image Works. p. 138 cr: © Thomas Zimmerman/FPG International Corp.; bc: © Bob Daemmrich/The Image Works. p. 139 bl: © R. Lord/The Image Works; tr: © Pedrick/The Image Works. p. 140 Lincoln: © Stock Montage Inc. p. 141 cl: © The Granger Collection; br: © Stanley Bach for Scholastic Inc. p. 142 cl: Carlo Ontal; bl: © UPI/Bettmann Archive. p. 143 tr: © Dan McCoy; cr: © courtesy of Clarion Books.

Illustrations: pp. 30-31: Paul Breeden; p. 46: Steve Meeks; pp. 72-73, 75-82, 84-89: Paul Schmid; pp. 102-107, 109: Keaf Holliday; pp. 127-128: Mary Keefe.